FINDING MONEY

FINDING MONEY

A Businessman's Guide to Sources of Financing

James G. Hellmuth

BOARDROOM® BOOKS, INC.

500 Fifth Avenue, New York, NY 10010

Fifty Dollars

Fourth printing.

Library of Congress Cataloging in Publication Data
Hellmuth, James G.
  Finding money; a businessman's guide to sources of financing.

  Includes index.
  1. Small business—United States—Finance.
2. Business enterprises—United States—Finance.
I. Title.
HG3729.U5H4   658.1'592'0973   80-14860
ISBN 0-932648-12-6

ACKNOWLEDGEMENTS

The author owes special thanks to the following for their assistance: Robert Bartlett and Lawrence F. Friess of the U.S. Small Business Administration; Marlin Aycock of the Farmers Home Administration, U.S. Department of Agriculture; Richard Sullivan of the Economic Development Administration, U.S. Department of Commerce; William D. Hassett, Jr., of the New York Urban Development Corporation; and James R. Boyle of the New York Job Development Authority. Particular thanks are due to Ogden Tanner for his patient and skillful editing.

Table of Contents

Chapter One

"GO WHERE THE MONEY IS"

Willie Sutton, one of the more successful bank robbers of modern times, once summed up his working philosophy in the pithy phrase: "Go where the money is." Though most entrepreneurs cannot be quite as direct in their methods as Willie, his advice is still sound when it comes to looking around for financing--particularly if everyone from your friendly banker to your in-laws has been noticeably cool.

In older, simpler days, when a businessman needed money he walked down the street to see his friend at the local bank on the corner, chatted awhile about the last Rotary meeting or the latest ball games--and as often as not came back to the office with a promise of a loan. Today, however, "where the money is" may not necessarily be the bank on the corner or, for that matter, any bank in town. In recent decades the money market has become a complex place, with dozens of different kinds of lenders and investors, both private and public, getting into the act.

Beyond commercial banks, the traditional financiers of businesses, funds for different purposes are available from savings banks, savings and loan institutions, credit unions; from finance companies, leasing companies, insurance and pension funds; from small business investment companies and venture capital firms; from public and private investors interested in offerings of company stock or debt; and, not least, from literally scores of federal, state, and local agencies set up to help companies looking for financial aid. You may even want to consider a relatively new financial wrinkle: setting up your own small business investment company. By financing your customers through such a setup you can help ensure their ability to pay you promptly and in full, thus reducing or eliminating your need to borrow outside funds (see Chapters 6 and 7).

Taken together, the proliferating money sources that exist today have uncounted billions of dollars in their coffers, waiting to be tapped by the right applicants at the right time. As a businessman you would do well to study the possibilities and limitations of as many of them as you can before you make a final decision on which to approach for funds.

Pinning Down the Amount

If your company is short of cash, the first thing, of course, is to determine exactly how much money is needed, over what period of time--and, if it is in the form of a loan, exactly how and when you will be able to pay it back. It is vital to pin down the precise amount of cash your business needs. If you obtain too little, your company may run short of money before it has met its objective, putting you in the embarrassing, and difficult,

4

position of having to ask for more. If you obtain too much, your company may be unnecessarily, even fatally, burdened with the cost of excessive borrowing, or your ownership needlessly diluted by the excessive equity you have sold.

Imprecision in presenting your financial needs may also be a dead giveaway to a potential lender or investor. He is bound to analyze your figures carefully, and chances are he will know more about the intricacies of financing and cash flow than you do. If you are vague about the amount or kind of funds you need, or exactly how you are going to spend them, he will chalk it off to poor planning--and he may begin to wonder how capable you are of handling other facets of your business too. Good management is the most important single attribute lenders and investors look for before committing money, and a company's financial operation is where they look first.

Regardless of what sources of money you consider, don't approach any until you have prepared a cash flow projection of your business for at least the next three years. As time passes this projection will compare, month by month, your budgeted cash flow and your actual cash flow (as it occurs). Your figures, based on the prior operations of your company and your best judgment of its future performance, are bound to be more accurate for the first projected year. But even though your projections for the second and third years may be less accurate, they will nonetheless be valuable, both to a prospective lender and to you, because they will force both of you to look well into the future with a realistic eye. A simple and direct way of drawing up a three-year cash flow projection is shown in the sample format on page 9.

Where to Get Sound Advice

Some businessmen are reluctant to discuss their financial matters with anyone, especially strangers, but often this is the best way to arrive at a sound decision about how much money a company actually needs, how much should be in the form of debt and how much in equity, and what the best sources of those funds might be. Most businessmen are experts in only one management area, like manufacturing or sales, and they need all the help they can get in the financial field--particularly in view of the fact that the money market is changing all the time.

Whether you get free advice or pay for it is not as important as who is giving it and the quality of the advice he is able to give. The ideal adviser is someone who understands your particular kind of business, with all its peculiarities and special problems, who has had some years of experience in financing businesses of your type and, if possible, is currently involved in the finances of companies of about your size. If you can find such a person, you are lucky; he may be willing to give you some answers without charge, either out of professional interest, generosity, or the chance that he may be able to do some business with you by lending to, or investing in, your firm. If you don't know someone with such qualifications, you may be able to find a good candidate through the offices of a financial adviser, either a friend in the financial business or a professional agent to whom you pay a fee (see Chapter 10).

The worst kind of advice, of course, is an opinion from someone who doesn't know what he is talking about--whether he be a fellow businessman whose experience has little to do with your own situation or a well-meaning but uninformed friend. There are several kinds of sources of advice,

6

however, that are both free and apt to be sound. These include many of the governmental agencies discussed in this book: the regional offices of the Small Business Administration, the Economic Development Administration, and the Farmers Home Administration. At the state, county, and municipal levels, other agencies can be helpful, including industrial development agencies and business development corporations that operate under a variety of names (see Chapter 9 for information on borrowing through state and local government agencies).

Still other sources of financial guidance include the Service Corps of Retired Executives, better known as SCORE, a national organization of experienced older businessmen from all kinds of fields who volunteer their management wisdom without charge. Another national group is the Active Corps of Executives, or ACE; it operates in much the same way but is composed of men and women who are still working in various businesses, professions, and educational institutions. Some states, and even a few cities, have established their own volunteer groups of executives, retired or active, who are in an especially good position to advise companies either in, or moving to, their regions. The Small Business Administration's Management Assistance Programs offer management and financial advice, while its Small Business Institute, established in cooperation with graduate schools of business administration in different parts of the country, offers further assistance to smaller companies that are located near the business schools. Faculty members as well as graduate business students make their expertise available to these firms without charge, gaining in return the opportunity to study specific business problems out in the field.

If at First...

The final ingredient in obtaining financial backing is perseverance, as it is in almost any field. Indeed, it may be the ultimate key if your ideas are ahead of the times, or if you have a product or service that you have faith in but that conventional lenders may regard as one without a future or involving too great a risk.

At the depths of the Depression in the 1930s, a young engineer-lawyer named Chester Carlson was working in the patent department of a New York electronics firm, had just gotten married and, like a lot of young men, felt he was not getting ahead fast enough. On his job, however, he had noticed that there never seemed to be enough carbon copies of patent specifications, and there seemed to be no quick or practical way of getting more. After months of evenings spent in research at the New York Public Library, he began experimenting with photoconductive materials in the kitchen of his apartment (much to his bride's distress), then moved his paraphernalia to a small laboratory in a rented room above a bar. One day in late 1938 Carlson and Otto Kornei, a young physicist he had hired to help him, hit on a crude method of making a visible image on a sulfur-coated plate by means of an electrostatic charge and exposure to light. After repeating the experiment several times to convince themselves it really worked, they closed up the lab and went out to celebrate.

Over the next five years Carlson pounded the pavements looking for a company that would finance his idea. He was turned down by more than 20, including some of the country's leading corporations in the fields of photography and office machines. Carlson had almost decided to drop the idea completely when he happened to sit next to a research engineer on an airplane flight and got to talking about his invention. Intrigued, the engineer in turn talked the Battelle Research Institute, for which he worked, into doing the development in return for future royalties. Battelle then entered into a contract with Haloid, a small photo-paper manufacturer in Rochester, New York, to produce and market a copying machine.

It was not until 1959--21 years after Carlson had invented xerography--that the first convenient, high-speed Xerox office copier was unveiled, signaling the emergence of a vast, worldwide copying industry whose products now seem as much a part of everyday business life as the typewriter and the telephone. Haloid, whose earnings had been $100,000 in the year it signed with Carlson and Battelle, became the Xerox Corporation, one of the most spectacularly successful companies in the history of American business, with sales in the billions and earnings of $500 million a year. Not surprisingly, Chester Carlson got the Horatio Alger Award--and a rather comfortable income for life.

FORM FOR A THREE-YEAR
CASH FLOW PROJECTION
(For 36 month period ending_____, 19__)

	January		February, etc.	
Operating Cash Receipts	Budget	Actual*	Budget	Actual*
1. Cash revenues	_____	_____	_____	_____
2. Collection of receivables	_____	_____	_____	_____
3. Other income	_____	_____	_____	_____
4. Total cash receipts	_____	_____	_____	_____

Operating Cash Disbursements	Budget	Actual*	Budget	Actual*
5. Raw materials				
6. Payroll				
7. Factory expenses				
8. Selling expenses				
9. Administrative expenses				
10. Advertising expenses				
11. Interest payable				
12. Taxes payable				
13. Total cash disbursements				
Net Operating Cash Balance (4 minus 13)				
14. Depreciation				
15. Investment and job credits				
16. Borrowing proceeds				
17. Sale of stock proceeds				
Total Cash Generated				
18. Principal borrowing repayments				
19. Plant & equipment expenditures				
Net Cash Position				
Cumulative Net Cash Position				

*Complete as they actually occur.

Chapter Two

TRYING THE BANKS ONE LAST TIME

Banks are much the most common sources of funds for businessmen, and for good reasons: they are the most numerous and widespread lending agencies; they are familiar with local businesses and trends; and they offer many different kinds of loans and other business services on competitive, government-regulated terms.

Banks, however, are just as well known for offering loans when you don't need them--and for looking at you with a glassy eye when you do. At one time or another, like most businessmen, you will probably go through the unsettling experience of asking your friendly banker for more money and getting an answer that, while it may be couched in the most cordial language, still amounts to a basic "No."

What then?

Probably the best advice anyone could give is: (1) go back to the drawing board and do a little extra homework; then (2) go back to your bank, or another one, well armed for a renewal of the fray. For even though you may have been turned down once, you should try at least one more time for bank financing before looking into other sources. You have nothing to lose and everything to gain.

What Went Wrong?

The first matter to explore, of course, is exactly why you were turned down. The loan officer may have concluded that you are not a good risk for repaying the loan because you are undercapitalized, or because you are already borrowing too much money to be able to handle the added repayments of a new loan. Or he may feel that your proposed use of the money is unbusinesslike or unwise. For example, he may wonder why you are buying a new plant for reasons of convenience or prestige when in his view your old one is perfectly adequate.

It may turn out that one of several other factors weighed in the bank's refusal. If your business is a relatively new one, you may not have established a sufficiently convincing "track record" to justify the risk. Or your business may be an old one--so old, in fact, that your banker believes your products will soon be out of date and no longer saleable. He may also be reluctant to lend money because he feels your field is overcrowded or that your business is part of an industry whose future is uncertain or already on the decline. The reason may be something as elementary as the fact that he may not rely on your accountant or his methods. Finally, the bank itself may be currently overextended, either in general loans or in loans to your particular kind of business.

12

Relationships Are Important

Many loan applications, however, are turned down simply because a bank's lending officers haven't known a particular businessman long or well enough to give him the benefit of the doubt in a borderline situation, or to give him the nod over a better-known applicant when the bank's lending funds are tight. So before going back to your present bank a second time, briefly review your past relationships. Do you have a personal acquaintance not only with the junior officer who may be handling your account but also with the senior officer or officers who pass on his recommendations? Have you invited them to visit your place of business to see your operation and meet your partners or key employees? (It is important for a new business in particular to demonstrate that it has some depth and breadth in management talent and is not strictly a "one-man shop.") Have you shown them all they want to know about your financial condition, how you run your business, and what the prospects for the future are?

Big Dividends: Free Ideas

As bankers are fond of pointing out, a continuing personal relationship with your banker is probably the most important intangible asset your business can have. And it is true that such a relationship can pay invaluable and sometimes unexpected dividends, not only in terms of loan money but of free ideas as well. In talking to other companies and examining their operations, sometimes in businesses quite unrelated to your own, a bank officer often comes across original and creative wrinkles in financing or accounting, in tax angles or government regulations, in production or sales techniques. If your banker knows you and your business intimately, and thinks well of them, it may occur to him to pass on an idea that you might have been unaware of and that could help you a great deal.

Sizing Up Different Types of Bank Loans

Remember, too, that a bank offers different types of loans, and while the type you first applied for may not have been possible for various reasons, with a little refiguring another type may suit you--and the bank-- just as well.

Obviously, the most desirable kind of loan, from the borrower's point of view, is an unsecured loan. With an unsecured loan, the bank's major security is its confidence in you as an entrepreneur and manager, in your skill and initiative, in your character and reputation, in the future of your business, and in your ability and willingness to repay the loan as it becomes due.

Credit Standing

A bank is only a general creditor under an unsecured loan, which means that it will move relatively slowly against a default, knowing it must stand in line with your other creditors. With an unsecured loan, too, your customers are apt to be more liberal in the credit they extend to your company than they would be if they knew that much of your assets were pledged as collateral to a bank.

A secured loan, however, gives the lender priority over the other creditors in the event of a default on the loan, and he may move quickly to exercise his lien, claim the collateral as his rightful property, and sell it at auction to recover the amount owed. This, of course, could be disas-

trous if the collateral pledged--such as basic manufacturing machinery--
is essential to the operation of your business.

If you can get one, an unsecured loan is best from your viewpoint and
the bank's as well. The interest rates are less because the bank considers
the credit of the borrower better and thus a lower risk to the bank; there is
also less paperwork involved in setting up the loan, and it is less time-
consuming and expensive to service over the period of its life. Remember
that the interest rate on a large loan, whether unsecured or secured, will
usually be lower than on a smaller loan, which brings in less money to the
bank but costs it just as much to research, set up, implement, and service.

A guaranteed loan is any loan in which a bank lends money only if a
third party agrees to guarantee repayment in case the borrower defaults.
This is a common situation covered in detail in other chapters; most of the
loan transactions entered into by the U.S. Small Business Administration,
for instance, are guarantees; banks actually furnish the money. If the
guarantor is not the government, however, the bank will ask to review the
guarantor's own financial statements to satisfy itself that he is capable
of stepping in and making good on the loan. If the bank considers your case a
borderline one, it may require not only that you secure the loan by putting
up sufficient collateral, but that you personally guarantee it as well--a
situation you should try to avoid if at all possible because your personal
assets will be on the line if for some reason your collateral becomes un-
available. This happened to more than one importer whose goods for the
Christmas season were trapped for more than two months aboard ships in New
York harbor because of a longshoremen's strike. While they had nothing to
sell during the season that traditionally accounted for two-thirds of

their profits, their overhead expense continued, forcing them into default on their loans. Since the next selling season was almost a year away, many lenders called their loans, requiring the importers to dig into their own pockets to make good on their personal guarantees.

Preparing Your Case

Regardless of the type of financing you hope to get, and whether or not the bank is familiar with your business, you can increase your chances immeasurably by submitting certain basic materials when applying for a loan. Many businessmen, though they may demand detailed information from their own suppliers or employees, are surprisingly naive when it comes to supplying the same kind of information to a bank. Then, when a banker asks unexpected and perhaps unwelcome questions to fill in the gaps, such businessmen become embarrassed or actually annoyed, believing they are being asked for privileged data that is really none of the banker's business and is not needed to make the loan.

A banker, however, has to know a great many details if he is to assess his risks properly and stand a reasonable chance of having his loan repaid, on time and in full. So before meeting with him, you should prepare the following written material (a few banks have their own detailed loan applications and prefer that the information be filled in on their own forms):

1. A short statement of how much money the company will need, for how long, and how it will be used (for working capital, plant modernization or expansion, an acquisition). This statement should also cover what security or collateral is available, and how the loan will be repaid.

2. A summary of the history and operations of the company. This should

include the type of business, its products or services, its legal organization (proprietorship, partnership, corporation), and the names of the principals and their education and experience. It should also outline how and where the company operates, how it stands in relation to its market and competitors, who its major customers are, and what percent they represent of its total business. Other information should cover the source and amount of the company's capitalization, its previous financing, credit rating, credit insurance for accounts receivable, "key man" insurance against the disability or death of managing principals. Also needed will be a description of plant and equipment, work force, whether unionized or not, and the status of a pension fund, if any.

3. Audited income statements for the past three years. (If you do not have audited financial statements, you can substitute copies of your company's federal income tax forms.)

4. Latest income statement for the current fiscal period, even if unaudited.

5. Audited balance sheets for the past three years, if available.

6. Latest balance sheet for the current period, even if unaudited.

7. Realistic income projections for the next three years.

8. Balance sheets projected for the next three years.

9. Cash flow projections for the next three years, showing the desired bank loan as made and as being repaid.

10. An outline of your company's backlog by contracts and products or services, including an estimated dollar total of the backlog and an estimate of production or services required to completely eliminate the backlog, assuming no new business is received.

Review all this material carefully to make sure it gives an accurate and honest picture of your business. If you have made a mistake in business judgment somewhere along the line, don't attempt to cover it up; point it out, state the circumstances, and show any corrective action taken. Most bankers are competent enough to spot "fudging"; they also know that if a businessman is smart enough to admit his errors he is probably smart enough not to make the same mistake twice.

Presenting Your Case

It goes without saying that any documentation you present to a bank should be well organized and neat. All material, of course, should be typewritten, and it will be far easier to read and handle if it is incorporated into a simple, attractive binder. (In a large bank, the senior loan officer having the ultimate say may not be present at the meeting; he may have to base his decision on the written material alone.) Where appropriate, include illustrations of your product, your building, or your assembly line; they can be worth the proverbial thousand words. If you can bring actual samples of your products to the meeting, so much the better; they can lend a note of reality that even the best pictures can't get across.

Schedule the presentation meeting well in advance, at a time that suits the convenience of the bank officers involved. Unless you feel totally qualified to answer any and all questions raised, plan on bringing along your financial man, whether he is an outside accountant or an in-house employee. Also plan to bring enough bound copies of your material so that everyone, including you and your advisers, can refer to the same figures at the same time.

18

Timing a Loan Application

When you apply for a loan can be as important as how you apply, both from your viewpoint and that of the bank. It is easiest to obtain any loan when (1) your company is doing well, and (2) when the bank has excess funds to invest. Ideally, you should apply at a time when these two circumstances coincide.

If you know your banker well enough you should be able to find out when the bank is likeliest to have money to lend. If you do not need the money immediately, but know that you will probably need it in the near future, it may pay you to take advantage of an upswing in sales and profits to make your loan application when the bank has funds available. Any excess funds for which you have no immediate use can be invested in savings accounts, certificates of deposit, or government notes, whichever offer the highest interest rates at the time. The difference between the interest charged on your loan and the interest paid from such investments will probably be small--smaller still when you consider it as a pre-tax expense of which the federal and state taxing authorities will be indirectly paying about half. For example, if you borrow $100,000 at 15 percent interest ($15,000) and invest it until needed in a certificate of deposit paying 13 percent ($13,000), the cost or difference to your company will be $2,000. If this is deducted from your company's pre-tax earnings it will reduce them by $2,000, but it will reduce your after-tax earnings by only $1,000 if your company's combined tax rate is 50 percent. The cost will be even less significant if you look on it as an inexpensive kind of insurance premium for having the extra funds on hand when you need them--at a time when the money market may be tight and loans difficult to obtain.

Trying a New Bank

If, despite careful preparation, timing, and presentation, your bank still will not approve the loan you want, you may be able to get it at a different bank. This can be another bank long established in your area, or it can be a newly chartered bank, a new bank created through the acquisition of an existing bank by another banking organization, or a new branch of an expanding chain. Any bank that is relatively new in town is an especially good prospect, since it will probably be more aggressive in its initial lending policies in order to build new business for itself; to compete with established local banks it is likely to be more liberal in approving loans and may be prepared to offer larger amounts and/or lower interest rates.

In approaching a second bank, first try to arrange an introduction to one or more of its officers through someone who knows them, preferably a person who is not only on friendly terms with you but who is also a good customer of that bank. Since you will have to explain and document your business to entirely new faces, ask for and allow sufficient time to prepare your case before an initial meeting at the bank. As a follow-up plan on inviting the officers involved to visit your place of business so they will have a chance to see your operation, meet your partners or key employees, and get their own impressions firsthand.

A New Bank vs. an Old One

Changing banks, while sometimes necessary, is a little like changing wives: loyalty and old ties must be weighed carefully against the glamour and promise of the new. A long and close working relationship with a sympathetic banker is not one to be severed lightly. He is not only in a position to help with financing when funds are available, but he can also provide sound business advice on a continuing basis, as well as special banking services in addition to your normal corporate checking account: letters of credit for foreign transactions and hedges against fluctuating foreign exchange; advice on company investments and on private or public offerings of your company's stock or debt; stock transfer and dividend-paying services once your stock is publicly held; various methods of speeding up collection of your accounts receivable and reducing clerical effort and expense.

Like many things in this changing world, unfortunately, the old-time personal relationship between an individual and his banker has tended to erode under the pressures of complexity and competition. Bank officers come and go with reassignments and promotions, with shifts from one bank branch to another, and with moves to entirely different banks. A new loan officer or lending policy at your present bank may contribute to a decision to turn down your loan application, or may result in a loan whose amount seems to you too small or whose interest rates seem too large.

If such turns out to be the case, the time may have come for you to "shop around," to look for another bank that will approve your loan or give you a larger loan at a more favorable rate. No matter how discreetly you do it-- and you should be reasonably discreet--it will probably be only a matter of time before your present banker learns through the grapevine that you have approached another bank. Don't be too concerned. He may not like it, but the odds are that he will accept it more readily than he might have 10 or 15 years ago. After all, he realizes just as well as you do that you have to borrow money wherever you can.

It is possible, of course, that both your old bank and a new one will be willing to approve a loan, the newer bank offering somewhat better terms. Unless the amount you need is so large that it can be split between the two, you will have to decide which bank to use. If you need only $300,000, say, a large bank with assets approaching $1 billion will probably not be very interested in sharing the loan with another bank. On the other hand, a smaller bank with assets of less than $200 million would probably not mind splitting the loan with another bank of similar size. If your borrowing needs exceed the legal lending limit of the bank you have been using, of course, you will have to seek out another bank that can handle the whole loan or is willing to split it with your present bank.

Past Performance and Current Capability

Don't stay with your present bank solely because of loyalty or old friendships; on the other hand, don't switch to a new bank solely because they offer better terms. There are many other factors to consider: how well your present bank has served you in the past; its range of services compared to that of the new bank; its record of interest rates charged by size of loans compared to those of the new bank; its requirement for demand deposits as a percentage of your borrowings in comparison to the percentage required by the new bank; its comparative record of involvement and commitment to your community and availability of funds for borrowers of your size when money is tight; and, not least of all, the personalities of the different officers involved and how well you think you could work with each.

Chapter Three

OTHER PRIVATE SOURCES OF FUNDS

If banks are unable to provide the financing you need, there are many other avenues you can explore. These range from approaching relatives and friends, trade credit, factors' loans, and lease-back plans to soliciting major investments in your company by venture capital firms.

Borrowing from Friends or Relatives

A main source of funds for small companies that are just starting out, or that are still in their early stages of development, is members of the owners' families and/or interested personal friends. One of the more spectacular American success stories features a young man named Walt Disney, who had gone bankrupt trying to start a film company in Kansas City and in 1923 moved to California to try it again. Disney and his brother Roy borrowed the modest sum of $500 from an uncle to begin a new enterprise aimed at making animated cartoons. The rest, of course, is history: from that original stake of $500, Walt Disney Productions grew to a corporation with annual revenues of well over $500 million and after-tax earnings of $100 million and more.

Not all family businesses turn out as happily, especially when disputes arise over who's in the driver's seat. In the 1930s three immigrant Irish brothers named Joyce obtained Midwestern bottling and distributing rights to a new soft drink named Seven-Up and eventually became millionaires many times over. Trouble broke out, however, when the brothers and their sons became involved in maneuverings to dominate the board. Haggling degenerated into hatred as the family split into two feuding factions, each convinced that the other was trying to do it in. Matters finally came to a grisly head (and a criminal trial) in 1977 when a mysterious dynamite blast wiped out a six-car garage on a family lakefront estate in the Wisconsin woods--permanently blinding one of the younger Joyce cousins and blowing a mysterious visitor from Chicago to bits.

Whether you bring your family or friends into your business is largely a personal matter--as you may discover it is in more than one sense of the word. A long-lost cousin, a doting aunt, or an old war buddy may trust you well enough to make a loan or buy some stock in the company, usually with a lot less investigation and paperwork than an institutional lender would require. But despite initial assurance of "wanting to help" and "not expecting it to be repaid," you may soon find yourself the target of all sorts of free advice from amateurs about the conduct of your business. And, when the chips are down, you can expect some surprisingly hard-nosed questions from family creditors about their money. At that point, you may decide that in the future, dealing with an "arm's length" investor or lender would be a wiser and more businesslike course.

Trade Credit

A major, indirect source of day-to-day operating funds, and one that more and more businessmen are utilizing to the fullest, is trade credit: buying raw materials, merchandise, equipment, or services on credit extended by the suppliers themselves. The longer the terms of the credit you can arrange, the longer you will have the use of your money for other purposes; your suppliers, in effect, will be making you short-term, interest-free loans. Over the past years three basic types of trade credit have come into use. The most prevalent is credit of the "open account" type; somewhat less common is a practice known as a trade acceptance; and the least widely used is a promissory note.

In an open account there is no formal acknowledgement of debt; the evidence lies in the purchase orders you give a supplier, in the entry of those orders in his books as accounts receivable and in your books as accounts payable, and in some cases signed shipping orders showing that goods have been received. For most businessmen used to dealing with each other, and who have reputations for reasonably prompt payment when payment is due, an open account is usually the simplest and the best.

In certain businesses--importing or exporting goods like coffee or scrap steel, for example--a supplier may draw up a trade acceptance, a document that you sign to indicate acceptance of its terms. The terms require you to pay the amount due by the date specified, usually 30 to 90 days, at a bank that you designate. The supplier may hold the acceptance to its maturity and cash it in for its face amount--the entire sum due--or he may immediately present the acceptance for payment at his bank and receive an amount discounted from the face amount. In any case, the acceptance eventually comes back to the bank that you designated to make the payment.

Formal, Immediate Evidence of Debt

A promissory note is favored in businesses like the fur or jewelry trade, whose undercapitalized suppliers like to have immediate evidence of debt so they can obtain additional working capital by discounting the note at the bank. A promissory note is a more formal acknowledgment of debt than a trade acceptance; in it, as a debtor, you make an unconditional, written promise to pay the amount due by a specific date at a designated bank, either to the supplier or any other holder of the note. Other holders are often banks that buy promissory notes at discounts as a form of investment, and they can look to either the supplier or the buyer for payment in the event of a default. The supplier, or someone else to whom he sells the note, may present it for early discounted payment, but, like a trade acceptance, it winds up in your bank's hands for payment on the specified due date.

The terms of any trade credit generally depend on the kind of services being rendered or the type of goods being sold. Service firms like accountants, automobile repair shops, and office-cleaning services expect to be paid on receipt of their bills, or at most within 30 days. Sellers of perishable goods with high rates of turnover also demand short credit terms. For example, wholesalers of fresh fruit, meats, and poultry like to be paid in full upon delivery. Manufacturers of durable goods, on the other hand, are willing to wait much longer because they run a minimal risk of the goods losing value during the period of payment. Sellers of seasonal goods such as toy manufacturers do not expect to be paid until weeks after they have delivered their toys for sale during the Christmas rush. Generally speaking, a company can anticipate trade credit of zero days from suppliers of perishable goods like flowers or vegetables to as much as 90 days from suppliers of books or toys.

Equipment Financing

If you wish to stretch out payments much longer than trade credit would allow you, another method of gaining added operating funds is to lease major pieces of equipment--manufacturing machinery, electronic hardware like computers, store fixtures, automobiles and trucks--or to buy them on an installment plan rather than tying up a lot of working capital in them. Paying for the right to use equipment without actually owning it has become common practice, especially in firms that are short of cash. If a company's credit rating is not high enough to obtain bank loans for purchasing equipment, in fact, the only alternative may be a plan under which the manufacturer or distributor of the equipment takes on the lending risk himself in order to sell his goods. Makers of costly equipment like large computers and of long-life equipment like store fixtures have come to accept the fact that they must often tie up their own capital through a financing or leasing plan in order to make their products affordable. Since under such plans they are still legally the owners of the equipment, they are in a relatively good position as creditors: they have the security of a so-called chattel mortgage on the equipment and stand ahead of other unsecured creditors of the company if things should go wrong. And they know that no company is likely to default, except as a last resort, on obligations involving equipment without which it could not continue to operate.

In addition to keeping limited company funds free for other needs, leasing equipment can help you avoid the cost of expensive replacements if the equipment becomes obsolete. For example, if you have a month-to-month lease on a printer attached to your computer and another kind comes along that does the job faster at less cost, you can terminate your lease on the earlier model and make a similar deal for the better and cheaper one. By leasing, too, you can have the use of certain pieces of equipment only for as long as you need them, instead of being stuck with them for the rest of their useful lives. If you need additional trucks for deliveries during the six busy weeks from Thanksgiving to Christmas, you can simply lease them for that period. Yet another advantage of leasing is the fact that your company can treat lease payments as costs when doing a job under a cost-plus contract; you cannot include in such contracts the cost of equipment you already own. Finally, and far from least, you may well find that the manufacturer-owner of a piece of leased equipment is more interested in servicing his own property, especially in emergencies, than if his product were owned by you.

Sale-Leaseback Financing

Under a variation of leasing, you may be able to sell some of your existing plant, machinery, or equipment to a buyer and then lease it back from him, thus converting capital tied up in fixed assets into liquid funds you can use for other needs. Among buyers who participate in sale-leaseback financing are leasing companies, banks, pension funds, and insurance companies. Others are individual investment companies or partnerships that have been set up as tax shelters for persons with large incomes subject to high personal tax rates (by buying a $500,000 building with a life of 25 years, for example, such an investor can take the depreciation on it as a tax-deductible expense of $20,000 per year against his other income). Sale-leaseback is a particularly advantageous method for you to consider if you have a fixed asset like a factory or machinery that has appreciated greatly in value because of inflation and is now worth considerably more than its depreciated value shown on your books.

In selling and leasing back such an asset, you lose the ownership rights to it and no longer receive the tax benefits from its depreciation; this is the trade-off you must make for obtaining the use of the capital from its sale. However, you can also have a clause written into the contract that gives you the option of repurchasing the asset at the end of the lease. In order for you to claim tax benefits from depreciation or taxes paid after repurchase, the IRS requires that the repurchase price be at least 15 percent of the price at which the asset was originally sold.

Mortgages

Another way to convert fixed assets into usable cash is to mortgage your business property to a bank or other institutional lender, or remortgage it if a mortgage already exists. Remortgaging is especially advantageous if your original mortgage has been largely paid off, or if your property has appreciated substantially in value because of inflation or because it has become a more desirable piece of real estate.

Although you won't receive as much money from mortgaging your plant as you would by selling it and leasing it back, your mortgage payments will be less than lease payments would be for the same dollar value because the lender will be assuming less risk. If your plant, for example, is worth $1 million, a lender might agree to give you a mortgage for 75 percent of its value, on some standard arrangement like 20 years at 10 percent. On the other hand, let's assume you sell your plant for the full $1 million in order to lease it back; the purchaser might take out a $750,000 mortgage and put up $250,000 of his own. In that case, he would not only have to pay off the mortgage but he would also have his own money at risk--and tied up--in your plant. To make the deal worthwhile for him, he would expect to receive lease payments from you that would not only cover his mortgage payments (principal and interest) but that would also repay a reasonable percentage on his $250,000 investment.

Factoring: Putting Accounts Receivable to Work

Many companies, particularly medium-sized ones that do not have adequate working capital, simplify their financial problems by selling their accounts receivable to factors or finance companies, some of which are departments or wholly owned subsidiaries of banks. There are basically two types of factoring--"maturity" and "advance."

In maturity factoring, the factor conducts his own investigation into the creditworthiness of your customers and decides which accounts receivable he is willing to buy. He then buys these accounts and assumes the responsibility of collecting the money owed as it becomes due under the terms of sale of your goods (usually 30 days). He performs the necessary accounting or record-keeping, assumes the risk of any bad debts, and pays you the money originally owed to you on the date it is due, whether he has collected it by that date or not. As a fee, the factor will generally charge you between 1 and 1.5 percent of the total amount of receivables, depending on the size and number of the accounts and their record of being paid on time. This fee is, in effect, like an insurance premium that assumes your accounts receivables will be paid.

In advance factoring, the procedure is similar except that (on completion of his investigation) the factor immediately advances to you what your accounts owe you as of a specified due date (usually 30 days later). The factor charges his usual fee of 1 to 1.5 percent of the total receivables plus interest on his advance, usually figured at an annual rate of 2.5 to 5 percent above the banks' prime rate. Such advances can come in particularly handy when you are short of working capital and need funds to fill existing orders.

Notification—A Big Consideration

In either type of factoring, the factor may notify your customers that you have assigned your sales invoices to him and that they are to send their checks to the factor instead of to you (this is known as "notification factoring").

Ideally, you may not want your customers to know that your receivables are being pledged to a third party. Such knowledge may jeopardize an otherwise healthy business relationship--and may raise questions about your own credit standing--but this is a price you may have to pay. If the idea does not appeal to you, try to arrange instead for "non-notification"

31

factoring, in which you assign your sales invoices to the factor but continue to receive payments from your customers and immediately forward their checks to him.

Borrowing from Finance Companies

Finance companies often make loans that are secured not only by accounts receivable but also by inventories, machinery, or equipment. Terms of agreements vary, but a finance company will usually lend between 60 and 80 percent of the value of accounts receivable, and between 50 and 60 percent of the value of inventories, machinery, and equipment. The worth of the collateral must be more than enough to cover its loans.

Interest rates vary with the credit standing of the borrower and also with the finance company's ownership. Independent finance companies, which must borrow a portion of their own funds from banks, usually charge interest of 3.5 to 5 percent over the banks' prime rate; a finance company owned by a bank, in contrast, has readier access to funds on more favorable terms and generally charges 2.5 to 4 percent over the prime rate.

Setting a "Cap"

A finance company may agree to lend you either a fixed or floating amount (usually with a "cap" or upper limit in the latter case), as long as your total receivables and/or inventories equal or exceed that amount. Let's say the company agreed to lend you $140,000, based on 80 percent of receivables worth $100,000 ($80,000), plus 60 percent of inventories worth $100,000 ($60,000). If your receivables dropped to $80,000 in a given period and your inventories grew to $150,000, the finance company would still lend you the original $140,000, because the total would be greater ($154,000--the sum of 80 percent of $80,000, or $64,000, and 60 percent of $150,000, or $90,000). If, on the other hand, your receivables dropped to $80,000 and your inventories to $80,000, the finance company would only lend you $112,000 instead of the original $140,000 because the total would be less ($112,000--the sum of 80 percent of $80,000, or $64,000, and 60 percent of $80,000 or $48,000).

When the loan is secured by accounts receivable, most finance companies prefer to have the accounts assigned to them, and do the collecting of the receivables themselves. This permits them to know the exact amounts outstanding and whether the accounts receivable are "good"--that is, being paid on time. This is a case when your customers will definitely be notified by the finance company that their accounts have been assigned-- and that their payments should be made to the lender instead of to you.

Insurance Companies and Pension Funds

Sources for long-term financing that are sometimes overlooked by businessmen include insurance companies and pension funds. It is not always a simple matter to obtain money from them; by nature they are cautious lenders and investors, and by law, for the protection of their policy holders and pensioners, they are tightly restricted in their investment activities. Under the Employee Retirement Income Security Act, for example, pension funds must follow the so-called "prudent man" rule, which in effect says that they can lend to, or invest in, certain kinds of business only if other "prudent" fund managers are doing so. As a result, few want to be pioneers in advancing money to small companies or those they consider to be in risky fields, but occasionally they will consider mortgages or sale-leaseback plans.

Though subject to the prudent-man rule, insurance companies have somewhat more latitude than pension funds, thanks to special programs and laws. Under the so-called "basket clause," first established in New York State, they are permitted to invest a small amount of their total assets, usually in the neighborhood of 3 or 4 percent, in situations that need not meet the otherwise stringent requirements imposed by state laws. You may obtain financing under this provision, particularly if you are willing to offer an insurance company the lesser risk of debt, or a combination of equity and debt, rather than the higher risk of equity alone. Both insurance companies and pension funds prefer to extend loans in the form of mortgages on real estate, usually for a term of 15 years or more.

It should be noted, however, that some insurance firms have seen the virtues of setting up their own special programs to aid businesses, through small business and minority enterprise investment companies like those discussed in Chapter 5.

Venture Capital Firms

These are among the organizations classed as venture or risk-capital firms. And if you believe that your company has something "special" about it--a particularly skilled management team, let's say, or a new wrinkle in a product or process that promises exceptional growth--you should consider the possibility of financing from such a source. Hundreds of these organizations exist in varying forms around the country. Some are owned by private investors or partnerships set up by wealthy individuals who are looking for unusual long-term profits. Others are institutional investors who pool some of their money with an eye to special situations. Still others include investment banking firms that from time to time form syndicates of investors to back promising ventures; and large corporations that invest in small companies to supplement their own research and development programs and keep up with technological breakthroughs in their fields.

In thinking about venture capital firms, it is important to recognize their difference from other kinds of investor-lenders. While bankers are primarily interested in a company's past record and its proven ability to generate sufficient cash flow to repay their loans, venture capitalists invest not for interest income but for substantial long-term capital gains. By purchasing stock in a company they believe has an extraordinary potential for growth, they hope to triple, or even quintuple, their money over a period that generally ranges from five to seven years. Since they are in a risky, high-stakes game, they are much more interested than a commercial bank in the novel features of a company's product or service, and in the size of the potential market and the company's chances of becoming a major factor in it. At the same time they place a premium on the competence and zeal of the company's management; they are not so much concerned as to whether or not the company has yet turned a profit, but whether it has experts in design, production, marketing, and other skills who are capable of making even a borderline product a commercial success.

Investors with Patience

If a venture capital outfit believes that both product and management give a company a definite competitive advantage, it may decide to invest in its future. The investors are quite willing to wait several years to see that future realized, but when it is they expect to cash in. At that time they may decide to take their capital gains either by selling the appreciated stock they own back to the company itself, by participating in an offering of the stock to the public at large, or by engineering a profitable merger with a larger firm.

Not everyone is successful in obtaining venture capital. A typical venture firm may receive as many as a thousand proposals in a given year-- and reject 90 percent of them because they lack intrinsic merit, because they do not fit the firm's policies or portfolio at the time, or simply because the proposals themselves are poorly documented and prepared. The remaining 10 percent are subjected to rigorous investigation: not only are budgets, plans, and projections carefully scrutinized, but a partner or executive of the firm may actually spend a week or two visiting the managers of a company in its offices and plant in order to size up the situation at first hand.

Most venture firms are interested in investments ranging from at least $250,000 to around $1.5 million (on occasion a firm may go much higher, as one did in investing $5 million in start-up money for the Amdahl Computer Company, now a competitor of IBM). On the other hand, smaller firms may consider lesser amounts. The percentage of equity a venture capital firm seeks in a company will vary, from as little as 10 percent in the case of a sizable, well-established, and profitable business to as much as 80 percent in the case of a promising company that is just starting out and may be having financial woes. Contrary to the anxious fantasy of many company owners, few venture firms want to "take control" of a business they invest in; the investors rarely have either the time or technical know-how to manage a number of different businesses in different industries, and prefer to leave control in the hands of each company's professional managers--the asset in which, after all, they are really investing. So that owner-managers will not lose their personal incentive to keep building their company, a venture firm will usually limit its participation to 30 or 40 percent of the ownership, exceeding 50 percent only if additional funds are required. Generally the financing will be in the form of preferred stock, debentures convertible into stock, or loans carrying options or warrants allowing them to be converted into stock at some future date, at a price agreed on in advance.

Their Man on the Board

Though it may maintain a largely "hands off" position in daily operating matters, a venture firm will undoubtedly want some say in major decisions on products, markets, and financing. For this reason it will probably ask that at least one of its partners or executives be made a member of the board (such a director, if he is knowledgeable, may well prove more helpful than anything else). To protect its investment, the firm will usually ask that covenants also be written into the financing agreement permitting the firm to take over and appoint new officers if serious problems should arise.

There is no exact formula for determining just how much of a company its owners would be wise to hang onto and how much they should sell to a venture capital firm. Only negotiation and compromise can produce the best agreement: one that gives the company funds for growth sufficient to offset its owners' loss of equity, and at the same time assures the venture investors of a stake that will grow fast and impressively enough to be worth their risk.

Making the Proposal

To be considered at all by a venture capital firm, you should have not only an attractive product or service but a carefully prepared proposal. This should include:

1. Your purpose: a clear and concise summary of what you are setting out to do.

2. How much money you will need, for what specific needs and in what form, not only initially but as the project moves along.

3. A description of your product or service, including cost details.

4. A marketing strategy, including the characteristics of the market, the competition, the market segment you presently have or plan to get, and your plans and estimated costs for attaining the goals you have in mind.

5. A brief history of your company, including its organization, past products, banking relationships, work force, employee relations, and any other pertinent information.

6. Biographical sketches that outline the business experience and qualifications of owner-managers and key employees.

7. How your company is capitalized: who its shareholders are, how much they have invested and in what form.

8. Financial statements for the past several years, and projections for the next three to five years showing what will happen if the desired financing is obtained.

9. Names and descriptions of your principal suppliers and customers, along with any special qualifications they may have.

10. A frank discussion of any contingencies or problems: liabilities, pending litigation, difficulties with taxes, patents, or the like.

11. A final statement of what you believe to be special about your case, whether it is an unusual product, a particularly good marketing scheme, or outstanding technical skills.

To find out what venture capital firms might be particularly good prospects in your region, or for the kind of business you are in, talk to knowledgeable members of the financial community in your town. In addition, you can consult written sources of research. The most comprehensive listing of firms is a book entitled Guide to Venture Capital Sources, published and periodically updated by Capital Publishing Corporation, P.O. Box 348, Wellesley Hills, MA 02181. It not only describes in detail each firm and the type and size of investments it prefers, but also provides a bibliography for further reading in depth.

Chapter Four

BORROWING FROM THE SMALL BUSINESS ADMINISTRATION

You are in a fix. Your business needs funds, but you can't borrow on reasonable terms from a bank, finance company, or other private source. Your options, however, are far from exhausted. Your next logical step is the Small Business Administration, which will probably be able to assist you with a loan or a loan guarantee. By law this agency cannot make any loan unless the borrower demonstrates that he has been unable to obtain funds from a bank or other private source; in cities of more than 200,000 population an applicant must show that he has applied to two banks unsuccessfully before he can apply for an SBA loan.

Since the SBA's inception under the Small Business Act of 1953, this agency of the U.S. Government has instituted more than a score of different loan programs and made well over a million loans with a total value of more than $36 billion; it has also guaranteed close to 200,000 surety bonds for contracts totaling more than $5 billion. In the process, it has helped all kinds of small businesses to get started, to grow and expand, or to offset disastrous losses.

The Rarest Loan

Basically the SBA assists businesses in one of three ways. The first --and least used--method is a direct loan, limited to a maximum of $350,000. Funds available for direct loans are usually in short supply and are made only to carefully selected borrowers, mostly disadvantaged entrepreneurs and the victims of natural or man-made disasters. Such loans may be made even when there is reasonable doubt of the borrower's ability to repay them, and the terms are exceptionally liberal, with low interest rates and generous maturities of 10 to 30 years.

Big Break on Interest and Maturity

A second, and more common, form of assistance is an "immediate participation loan," made in conjunction with a private lending institution like a bank. If a company, for example, needs $200,000, the bank may lend $100,000 and the SBA the other $100,000 (the SBA total share is limited to $350,000).

Advantages:

• The interest rate on the SBA's share is favorable (considerably lower than the prevailing market rate) and the rate on the bank's share is slightly lower than normal.

• The loan may run for 10 to 30 years in contrast to the normal bank loan of three to five years.

Solid Banking

The third, and most easily obtained, type of SBA financing is an SBA-guaranteed loan, issued when ordinary financing is not otherwise available on reasonable terms. The loan is made by a bank or other lending institution and guaranteed by the SBA up to a maximum of 90 percent of the amount or $500,000, whichever is less. All three types of SBA financing generally require a longer waiting period for approval than an ordinary bank loan, commonly four to eight weeks, and they may be restricted to a specific purpose such as the purchase of machinery, equipment, or buildings. As in the case of ordinary loans, the better the borrower's credit, the less restrictive an SBA loan will be.

Types of SBA Loans

The Small Business Administration makes--or guarantees--loans to businesses for almost any legitimate purpose; to construct, expand, or convert facilities, to purchase equipment or materials, or simply to obtain needed working capital. But it will not:

• Make loans intended to pay off inadequately secured creditors, to finance real estate investments, or to be used for speculation in any kind of property.

• Lend money to most non-profit organizations (exceptions in cases of disaster are discussed on page 48), to enterprises engaged mainly in lending or investing, or to those whose primary income is derived from gambling. Also, rather than risk accusations of attempting to control freedom of speech under the Constitution's First Amendment, the SBA excludes newspapers, magazines and book-publishing companies from its regular business loan programs, though they may qualify for disaster loans; radio, television, and cable TV companies are eligible on grounds that they are already federally controlled through the FCC.

How Big Is "Small"?

To be eligible for an SBA loan, your company must be independently owned and operated, it must not dominate its field, and it must meet certain standards of maximum size. These standards are under constant review with an eye to types of businesses within a given industry, to competition within a given category, and to increases in size and dollar volumes brought on by expansion and inflation. Standards governing size are as follows:

• Manufacturing--Any firm with 250 or fewer employees. Firms in certain types of manufacturing, such as man-made cellulose fibers, may have up to a maximum of 1,000 employees. To determine the maximum number of employees allowable in your category, consult your local SBA office for the schedules in Title 13 of the Code of Federal Regulations. (The 96 SBA field offices are listed with addresses and telephone numbers in Appendix B.)

• Wholesaling--Firms with yearly sales not exceeding $9.5 to $22 million, depending on the Title 13 size schedule for the particular kind of wholesaling involved.

• Retailing--Maximum annual sales between $2 and $7.5 million, depending on the type of retailing involved.

• Service businesses--Annual receipts not exceeding $2 to $8 million, depending on the service involved.

• General construction--Annual receipts not exceeding $9.5

million.

- Special trade construction (plumbing, electrical, air conditioning, painting, etc.)--Annual receipts of $5 million or less.

- Agriculture--Annual receipts of $1 million or less.

The size limits of firms eligible for SBA-guaranteed surety bonds are the same as those for loans, with two exceptions: neither general construction nor special trade construction firms may have annual receipts of more than $3.5 million.

For all industries, size standards are increased by 25 percent when companies are located in areas of substantial unemployment, underemployment, or redevelopment as defined by the Department of Labor. For example, a service business with annual receipts of $9 million would not normally qualify under the general $8 million ceiling for that industry, but if it were located in an area of substantial unemployment--New York City, Detroit, Newark, New Jersey, El Paso, Texas, or Mobile, Alabama, for example--the ceiling would be raised by 25 percent to $10 million.

Regular Business Loans

Regular business loans--direct, participatory, and guaranteed account for approximately $24 billion of the total $36.4 billion of loans made by the SBA. Loans for working capital are made for seven to 10 years; for machinery and equipment, 10 years or the life of the item, whichever is less; for the conversion or expansion of plant, and/or for land, a maximum of 20 years or the life of the plant, whichever is less. If a loan is made for both equipment and plant, its date of maturity is figured in relation to the loan dollars allocated to each.

Seasonal Lines of Credit

A loan program is also available to eligible small firms that need increased working capital due to substantial seasonal swings in their business. Such loans are not the customary revolving lines of credit and must be repaid within 12 months. A company can then apply for a second seasonal line of credit loan, but only after a 30-day waiting period following payoff of the existing loan.

The SBA will only make guaranty loans under this program. It will guarantee a maximum of $500,000 or 90 percent of a seasonal line of credit extended by a bank; under the so-called economic opportunity loan program available to disadvantaged borrowers (page 46), the maximum is $100,000 or 90 percent of the seasonal line. However, loan security is not automatic. In addition to the SBA guarantee, the bank can usually require that a company's accounts receivable and inventory be pledged to the bank as collateral for the loan.

Contract Loans

Another short-term type of loan is available to aid small building, manufacturing, and servicing firms that cannot perform under their contracts without additional funds. The SBA will only make guaranteed loans under this program, and the funds borrowed in this way can be used only for labor and materials. The contract is usually assigned to the bank as security for the loan. The applicant must have been in operation for the 12 months preceding the date of the application, and the loan must be repaid within 12 months. The SBA will guarantee up to $500,000 or 90 percent of the bank's loan.

Pool Loans

Under another available but little-used program, a group of business concerns may pool interests to form a corporation eligible for SBA loans. Such a corporation can take advantage of economies in joint buying of raw materials, supplies, or equipment, in cooperative research and development, or in construction of facilities to be shared by all. To satisfy anti-trust law requirements, the formation of such a pool must be cleared by the Department of Justice and notice furnished to the Federal Trade Commission. Each business in the pool may borrow up to $250,000 over a maximum period of 10 years (20 years if the money is used for construction). The loans may be direct, participatory, or guaranteed; rates and size standards for eligibility are the same as for regular SBA business loans.

Economic Opportunity Loans

In addition to regular business loans, the SBA has a number of special loan programs for which many companies may qualify. Some $1.3 billion of the loans made under SBA programs have been accounted for by so-called economic opportunity loans. These are made to socially or economically disadvantaged entrepreneurs who live in areas where there are high proportions of unemployed or low-income individuals, or who are members of ethnic minority groups, including blacks, American Indians, and Americans of Hispanic or Oriental extraction. An economic opportunity loan—participatory or guaranteed—of up to $100,000 may be made for working capital, for purchase of machinery, equipment, or land, or for construction, conversion, or expansion of plant. The maturity is a maximum of 15 years, regardless of the purpose of the loan. Most loans made under this program are direct loans from the SBA, with interest set at the government's own cost of borrowing. Applicants must be of good character, and it is important that they be able to demonstrate a reasonable assurance of repayment, but their credit does not have to be as high as that required for regular business loans.

Handicapped Assistance Loan Program

Another special loan program is designed to assist any non-profit organization in which at least 70 percent of the man-hours are accounted for by physically handicapped individuals, or any profit-making small business concern that is entirely owned by a handicapped person. SBA will make a direct loan of up to $100,000 at only 3 percent, a participation loan of up to $150,000 at a maximum of 11 percent, or guarantee as much as 90 percent of a guaranty loan up to the $350,000 maximum. Eligibility and criteria are the same as for a regular business loan, but in borderline cases where the applicant's ability to repay the loan is in doubt, the decision is generally made in his favor. The vast majority of the $78 million worth of loans made under this program have been direct loans.

Disaster Loans

The SBA is very much in the business of helping the victims of natural or economic catastrophes. For physical losses suffered from floods, hurricanes, tornadoes, and riots, loans are available to replace damaged physical assets. Any business, regardless of size, is eligible, as are such non-profit organizations as churches and schools, farmers who have lost their crops, and ordinary householders who have suffered damage to their homes. The amount of each loan is based upon the actual losses suffered; the collateral required is whatever may be left.

For a disaster loss sustained by a business or non-profit organization, the SBA will make a direct loan, or participate in a bank loan, up to a limit of $500,000. On a guaranteed loan there is no limit except the amount of the damages; SBA guarantees its customary 90 percent of such a loan. On a lost or damaged home the SBA will lend up to $50,000 on a direct or participation basis, and up to $10,000 to replace furniture and other personal effects, with a combined limit of $55,000; in the case of a guaranteed loan there is no limit except the damages suffered. Loans may extend up to 30 years, and interest rates are the same as for regular business loans. If the damages amount to more than 30 percent of an individual's total assets, he may also refinance his existing debt with an SBA loan. More than 700,000 loans totaling $7 billion have been made under this program--200,000 of them, worth $1.5 billion, as a result of Hurricane Agnes, which hit the Northeast, primarily Pennsylvania and New York, in June 1972.

Help for Businesses When the Damage Is Indirect

Under a separate program the SBA may also make loans to small businesses that have suffered hardship when normal business has been disrupted as a result of a natural disaster. There are no statutory limits on such loans, which are governed by the amount of economic loss; eligibility and interest rates are similar to those of regular business loans and terms may run up to 30 years. After the Mississippi floods of 1958, the SBA provided such assistance to cotton processors, grocery stores, and other businesses as well as to farmers who lost their cotton crops--the basis on which

48

the entire local economy depended. In all, some 7,500 loans of this type have been made for a total of $350 million, all but $6 million in the form of direct loans.

Displaced Business Loans

Businesses that suffer economic injury from federal, state, or locally assisted construction projects can also apply for SBA loans. If a manufacturer or retailer, for example, is forced to relocate because a highway or housing project preempts his site, he can borrow an amount beyond the condemnation price he receives in order to cover added costs: replacement value, cost of moving, cost of interruption to the company's operations. Some $450 million in such loans have been granted or guaranteed to date.

Economic Injury Loans

Similar programs have been set up to deal with losses suffered by businesses as a result of complying with standards established under various government health and safety acts. One of the most commonly used programs covers companies that have to make substantial additions or alterations to their plants or methods of operation to meet requirements imposed by the Occupational Safety and Health Act of 1970. Loans are made to offset the cost of improvements, but cannot be used for working capital. They may take the form of direct, participatory, or guaranteed loans; eligibility standards and interest rates are the same as for regular business loans made by the SBA and maturities can run up to 30 years. There is no statutory limit on the amount of the loan, which is determined by the extent of actual economic injury suffered by the company.

Other programs of like nature cover businesses that incur substantial costs in complying with the Clean Air Act of 1979, the Water Pollution Control Act of 1972, the Coal Mine Health and Safety Act of 1969, the Egg Products Inspection Act of 1970, the Wholesome Poultry and Poultry Products Act of 1968, and the Wholesome Meat Act of 1967. Still other programs are designed to aid small businesses that suffer from the closing--or reduction in operations--of a nearby major military installation, or from international treaties that limit the production or installation of strategic arms or missile bases. Loan funds can be used to help such businesses continue operations, move to a new location, buy another existing business, establish a new business, or refinance indebtedness.

A special program of "product disaster" loans is available to small businesses in food products industries that have been unable to process or market a product because of disease or toxicity brought about by natural or unusual causes. For example, an entrepreneur engaged in fishing for--or canning--swordfish could apply for a loan if his business were brought to a halt by the discovery of toxic concentrations of mercury in the fish (a manufacturer or supplier of cans to the processor, however, would not be considered directly involved and would not qualify for a loan).

Energy Loans

Under a relatively new program, established in 1974, small businesses can also seek assistance from the SBA if an energy shortage cripples, or threatens to cripple, them. The crisis may be direct--a lack of fuel or electrical energy; or indirect--a lack of needed raw or processed

50

materials resulting from the fuel or energy shortage.

In January 1979, the SBA began helping small businesses engaged in the energy systems field, either in developing energy-conserving products or devices like solar heating and wind-powered generators or in manufacturing, selling, installing, or servicing them. Eligibility amounts, rates, and other requirements are similar to those for regular business loans, except that the SBA is willing to take a greater risk on a company's credit standing, placing its emphasis on the technical soundness of the product or process and the technical qualifications of the applicant. In the first three months alone, more than $4 million in loans were approved. The program, backed by the Department of Energy's commitment to develop alternate energy-saving systems, promises to be even more active in the future.

Economic Dislocation Loans

Another innovative program, established in 1979, promises to assist small businesses that have suffered substantial injury as a result of so-called economic dislocation, generally caused by a shift in the purchasing power of their customers. Retailers in Texas towns near the Mexican border, for example, recently found that Mexican citizens who had been crossing the border daily to purchase goods in their stores stopped doing so because their purchasing power in the United States had been suddenly and drastically reduced by a Mexican devaluation of the peso. Some store owners petitioned the Administrator of the SBA, who determined that an economic dislocation existed and that they were eligible for special small business loans, up to a limit of $100,000 with a maturity of 30 years.

Surety Bond Guarantees

In addition to its various loan programs, the SBA is authorized to back up certain bonding arrangements. The agency can assist building and service contractors by guaranteeing up to 90 percent of the losses of a private surety bonding company resulting from a breach of terms of a bid bond, payment bond, or performance bond by the contractor. Any contract up to $1 million may be covered provided that:

1. The principal is a small business firm as defined by SBA standards.

2. The bond is required in order for the firm to bid on a contract, or to serve as a prime contractor or subcontractor.

3. The firm is not otherwise able to obtain such a bond on reasonable terms and conditions without a guarantee.

4. The SBA determines that there is a reasonable expectation that the firm will carry out the covenants and conditions of the contract, and that the contract meets SBA requirements for successful completion and reasonable cost.

5. The terms of the bond are reasonable in light of the risks involved and the extent of the bonding company's participation.

If a surety bond is guaranteed, a fee of $2 per $1,000 of the contract's face value is paid by the contractor to the SBA. In the case of a partial bond, the SBA's fee is $2 per $1,000 of the face value or 20 percent of the premium charged by the surety company, whichever is less.

To obtain an SBA guarantee for a surety bond, first consult a bonding agent or broker. If he determines that your company cannot obtain a bond on its own, he will advise you to seek assistance through the SBA Surety Bond

Guarantee Program. The SBA supplies agents and brokers with the two forms that must be filed: an Application Form and a Statement of Personal History. After you have completed these forms, the agent or broker will submit them simultaneously to the surety company and the SBA regional office. If the surety company decides to issue a bond with a guarantee, it then asks the SBA to review the request, a process that generally takes not more than a week.

Applying for an SBA Loan

The procedure for applying for all other SBA assistance--including direct, participatory, and guaranteed loans--involves documentation not unlike that required for an ordinary loan from a bank--another reason to hang onto the carefully prepared material from your last bank-loan application. In any case, SBA advises all applicants to talk first to their bankers, and to submit the following items:

1. A business plan consisting of a brief history of the business and its problems, including an explanation of why the loan is needed and how the money will be used to help the business.

2. An itemized cost estimate for all equipment and leasehold improvements to be purchased with the loan money.

3. Personal resumes of the owners of the business.

4. Signed balance sheets and profit and loss statements current within 90 days and for the last three fiscal years.

5. Federal income tax returns for the owners of the business for the last two years.

6. A copy of the lease on the business offices or other real estate or

a letter from the landlord with the terms of the proposed lease.

7. A copy of the Certificate of Doing Business (registration of the business with the County Clerk). If the business is incorporated, stamp the corporate seal on the application form.

8. A detailed projection of earnings starting with the first year of business operation. Be sure to explain how the expected sales volume will be achieved.

9. A list of available collateral to be offered as security for the loan with your estimate of the current market value of each item. (Collateral items might include mortgages on land, building, equipment, or chattels, warehouse receipts for marketable merchandise, and guarantees or personal endorsements.)

10. Personal financial statements of any partner or stockholder owning 20 percent or more of the company's corporate stock.

If the bank is willing to approve a loan on an SBA participation or guarantee basis, it will submit your material to the nearest SBA office with its comments and recommendations. The SBA will then either approve or disapprove the loan and notify the bank of its decision. If the SBA is unwilling to approve a bank loan, you can contact the nearest SBA office and inquire about the possibilities of a direct SBA loan.

If your request for a loan is for a new business, the procedure for applying is identical except that the material submitted must describe in detail the following:

• The type of business to be established.

• The experience and capabilities of management.

• An estimate of how much you and your shareholders will invest and how much you will need to borrow.

• A detailed projection of earnings for the company's first year of operations.

As with any application for financing, the better your presentation, the better chance you will have of obtaining your loan.

Chapter Five

GETTING FUNDS FROM A SMALL BUSINESS INVESTMENT COMPANY

For many businessmen, "where the money is" has proved to be a growing number of small business investment companies, or SBICs. These privately organized and privately managed firms are specifically licensed, and partially financed, by the federal government's Small Business Administration to provide equity capital, long-term loans, and management counseling to new or expanding firms. Since they were first authorized by Congress under the Small Business Investment Act of 1958, SBICs have made more than 50,000 loans to and investments in businesses, to the tune of well over $2.5 billion dollars.

There are more than 400 SBICs of all shapes and sizes scattered across the United States, and one or two new ones are formed every month. Together they represent a pool of some $1.25 billion available for investing or lending.

In Business to Make Money

It should be kept in mind that SBICs are genuine businesses in their own right, looking for profits just as you do. To generate capital gains for themselves, most SBICs are keenly interested in sharing directly in the profits of a growing business by buying common stock or convertible debentures or making loans with warrants to purchase stock. The terms of such transactions, too, are regulated by the SBA; SBICs are generally prohibited from taking a controlling position in a firm. And they can be as helpful with ideas as they are with money. Since an SBIC's ultimate success depends on the growth and profits of the companies in its investing portfolio, it frequently offers them management advice and services--a bonus that few businessmen are aware of at first but that in many cases has proved as valuable as the financing itself.

Fortunately, most businesses are now eligible to take advantage of SBIC financing: not long ago, the largest business that could qualify as "small" was one whose total assets did not exceed $9 million, but the SBA has recently liberalized the regulations to read "unlimited assets," and has raised the ceiling on net worth from $4 million to $6 million and the limit on after-tax earnings from $400,000 to $2 million.

What Defines an SBIC?

Basically, all SBICs operate under the same rules. Rigorously screened before they are licensed, they must raise a minimum amount of capital on their own before they can qualify for additional long-term loans from the SBA of up to four times their private funds (Chapter 7 describes the formation of an SBIC).

Under this broad umbrella there are two general types of SBICs. The most common is the regular or Section 301 (c) SBIC; more than three-quarters of all SBICs are of this kind, representing private funds totaling close to $550 million and SBA loans of nearly $640 million. The other type, organized under the slightly more liberal terms of Section 301 (d) of the Act, is the Minority Enterprise SBIC or MESBIC. Licensed solely to assist small businesses that are 50 percent or more owned by American blacks, Indians, Eskimos, and those of Hispanic or Oriental extraction, MESBICs also serve economically disadvantaged firms located in depressed urban and rural areas afflicted by low average incomes and high unemployment rates. More than 100 MESBICs are in operation, with total private funds of about $80 million and more than $90 million in outstanding SBA loans.

Of the regular SBICs, the largest single category comprises firms that are owned by individuals or small groups of local investors; others are owned by nonfinancial businesses organizations; still others belong to such financial organizations as finance companies and investment companies organized under the 1940 Investment Act. Some are listed as "bank dominated" (owned 50 percent or more by commercial banks); these represent the category with the highest total capital, more than $175 million. An additional few, with a capitalization of some $15 million, are "bank associated" (10 to 49 percent owned by banks). Some of the largest SBICs are publicly owned and their stock is publicly traded. The private capitalization of SBICs varies from less than $300,000 to more than $5 million; most are in the $300,000 to $1 million range.

All these SBICs (as well as the 100-odd MESBICs) are listed alphabetically by state in the Appendix beginning on page 132, along with their principal officers, addresses, and telephone numbers, their investment policies and types of ownership. You will note under "investment policy" that most list themselves as "diversified"; this means that they are licensed to lend to--or invest in--a wide range of businesses. In practice, many narrow the bulk of their portfolios to fields with which they are especially familiar. A smaller number of SBICs are limited by their licenses to specific areas in which they have special knowledge and competence. These areas indicated under "investment policy" include real estate construction, grocery stores, lodging and recreation, motion pictures, radio and TV, high technology, printing, health, energy, water transportation, even taxicabs and mobile homes.

What Kinds of Financing Do You Get?

An SBIC may meet your company's needs either by a straight loan, a stock investment, or a combination of the two. In the case of a loan, its cost, including the interest rate, is determined by negotiation between you and the SBIC but cannot exceed 7 percent per annum above the latest rate set by the Federal Financing Bank for 10-year money. The SBIC may require some form of collateral. You may have to agree to a lien on your assets (discuss this with any bank that is already financing you so the SBIC will not be ahead of the bank on any claims). You may also be asked to give a personal guarantee; try to avoid this, because if your company is unable to repay the loan in full you will have to dig into your personal assets to make up the balance.

When an SBIC Comes Aboard

In addition to or instead of a loan, chances are that any SBIC you approach will seek to make a direct investment in your company in order to increase its own potential profit through long-term capital gains.

Such an arrangement, like most deals, has its pros and cons. On the positive side, you will receive the money you need without being burdened with regular interest and principal payments as in the case of a loan; however, you will have to relinquish part of your own company's future profits to satisfy the SBIC investors. Under the circumstances, the most advantageous kind of stock for you to issue is common stock on which you do not have to pay out dividends. The SBIC, however, will almost certainly request that you issue it dividend-paying preferred stock because it is not required to pay income taxes on regular dividends (as explained in Chapter 7, SBICs may deduct from earnings 100 percent of dividends received from investments in their portfolio companies, instead of the usual 85 percent that other investing firms are allowed). Holding preferred stock also puts an SBIC in a safer position than that occupied by common stockholders; in the event of liquidation, preferred stockholders outrank them when the remaining capital is divided up.

Combinations

Many SBIC financings combine both loan and stock transactions. Here is how a typical combaination might work:

Assume that you and an SBIC agree that your need for $400,000 in overall financing is best met by a combination of $100,000 of common stock and a $300,000 loan. One way to handle this would be to break up the stock into 10 units of $10,000 each and the loan into 10 units of $30,000 each; if the SBIC is unable to furnish all the funds it might purchase five units of stock and debt and suggest that the other five be sold to another SBIC.

Frequently an SBIC will ask that the loan portion of the package carry warrants entitling it to purchase additional stock, or that the loan be in the form of a convertible debenture entitling it to convert a specified portion of the loan into common stock at an agreed-on price at any time during the life of the loan.

In such dealings with an SBIC, remember that the more profitable you think your company will become, the less equity in it you should give up in the form of stock, warrants, or convertible debentures. For example, if your company is currently earning $50,000 a year after taxes and in five years you expect it to be earning $200,000, a good practice would be to value the company at five times its future earnings, or $1 million. Rather than give up 25 percent, say, of these earnings to an SBIC in its equity investment, a more reasonable figure might be 10 percent, or a maximum of $100,000 in equity. Bear in mind, however, that the better position an SBIC can get on the equity portion of the package, the more likely it is to give you a lower interest rate on the loan portion. Conversely, the better interest rate the SBIC can get on the loan portion the more likely it will be to accept a lesser stock position on the equity portion of the package.

Advantages of SBIC Loans

In borrowing from any SBIC, you stand to gain in a number of ways, including the following:

• Longer terms. Under SBA regulations any financing must have a minimum maturity of five years, in contrast to normal bank or finance company loans, which may have to be paid back in a much shorter period.

• Lower rates. You cannot be charged more than 7 percent annually above the Federal Financing Bank's latest rate for 10-year money for financing, including interest, discounts, fees, commissions, and other charges--a figure that can reach 22 percent or more with other lenders. (An SBIC, however, may charge you separately for management services as long as the charges are comparable to those of established professionals.)

• Painless prepayment. You may pay off your loan at any time before the maturity date without paying a penalty, in contrast to the usual penalties imposed by other lenders for prepayment of term loans.

• Assured control. Still another advantage of SBIC financing is that any SBIC with which you deal is prohibited by law from taking effective control of your company: it cannot own, directly or indirectly, 50 percent or more of your outstanding voting stock, or more than 25 percent if such a block would represent an amount as large or larger than the largest other block of voting stock. (Potential ownership by the SBIC through stock options, warrants, or conversion privileges is not considered in determining whether a presumption of control exists; present ownership is what counts.) In the event of a default, however, temporary control of your company may be permitted if it becomes necessary for the participating SBIC to protect its loan or investment; in such an event the SBIC must file a plan, for SBA approval, relinquishing control later on, and a statement that both your company and the SBIC consider the plan fair.

Limits on SBIC Financing

Both SBICs and MESBICs are somewhat restricted in what they can do. An SBIC is not allowed to disburse more than 20 percent of its own capital (30

62

percent in the case of a MESBIC) to any one business firm. If you approach an SBIC with total private assets of $1 million, for example, you cannot expect it to lend or invest more than $200,000 in your company. However, two or more SBICs are permitted to participate in a single financing and thus provide a larger amount than any one could alone. If your company needed $400,000, you could approach a second SBIC to obtain the additional $200,000.

There are also limits on the types of businesses in which SBICs can invest. An SBIC cannot help your company if your own primary business is lending money (e.g., a bank or finance company), or if you are mainly engaged in financial activities, such as investing, factoring, purchasing debt obligations--or even leasing equipment without providing for its maintenance and repair. SBICs are prohibited from making loans to, or investments in, companies whose main revenue comes from gambling. Nor can they disburse funds intended for use outside the United States, though they can invest in a business that conducts some foreign operations as long as the major portion of its activities and assets remains within the U.S. Unless an SBIC is specifically licensed to specialize in firms engaged in real estate or motion picture production and distribution, it cannot use more than one-third of its total assets to finance businesses in those fields.

Selecting an SBIC

In looking around for one or more SBICs to finance your company, try to find those whose locations, interests, and capabilities match yours as closely as possible. As you consult the list in the Appendix, consider these factors:

• Geography. Generally, an SBIC is more likely to make loans and investments reasonably near its own place of business, though some operate on a regional or national basis and others headquartered far away may have a branch office in your area. A good start is to check out firms listed under your state or a neighboring state.

• Industry specialization. Ideally an SBIC should have some familiarity with your type of business, particularly if you plan to call on it not only for money but also for management advice. If a firm lists itself as "diversified," find out what this really means. At the same time, check the listings to see what firms have a stated area of specialization; if you are in the retail grocery business, for example, an SBIC dealing only in grocery stores may be a good bet even if its headquarters is located several hundred miles away.

• Investment preferences. Although most SBICs have both straight loans and equity investments in their portfolios, most also have their own policies governing the type of financing they offer. Before approaching any firm you should have at least a general idea of whether you want all your money in the form of a loan, a stock purchase, or a combination of the two, and in roughly what proportions. On this point and others, the regional or Washington office of the Small Business Administration can usually help steer you to firms whose interests coincide with yours.

• Amount of financing. Remember that no SBIC is allowed to invest more than 20 percent of its total private capital (30 percent in the case of a MESBIC) in a single business concern. If you need $400,000, you will have to find a firm with a total capitalization of $2 million--or develop a team of SBICs, which often are permitted to work together to make loans and stock

64

purchases in larger amounts than any one could accomplish alone.

• Management services. Many SBICs offer management advice on a fee basis. If you are likely to need assistance in shepherding your company as it grows--financial planning, advice on computer utilization, insurance, pension plans, etc.--make sure that the SBIC you are considering is capable of providing such services.

Shopping for the Right Outfit

In your search for an SBIC to fit your particular needs, don't hesitate to shop around. In addition to talking with the regional office of the SBA, consult your banker, your attorney, your accountant, and knowledgeable business associates and friends; you may well find one who has done business--or may even be associated--with an SBIC. Or you may be able to find someone who is an acquaintance of officers of an appropriate SBIC and is willing to introduce you. Such an introduction can serve as a character reference and make your first meeting more productive and relaxed.

If it seems likely that your interests will coincide, the next step is to prepare a report as you would for a bank loan (Chapter 2), outlining your operation, finances, and requirements, and including information on products, patents, markets, and key personnel. In most situations any SBIC you talk to will give you a quick reaction; the more clearly you document your case, the swifter and more favorable that reaction should be.

Chapter Six

IF YOU CAN'T SUCCEED AS A BORROWER-BE A LENDER (UNCLE SAM CAN HELP)

Are you short of working capital?

Are some of your customers also short of working capital?

Are your company's sales and profits suffering as a result?

Far from borrowing money yourself in order to plug these holes, the best way to solve all three problems simultaneously, strange as it may seem, may be to make loan funds available to your customers--and at bargain rates--through an SBIC. For this purpose, such an SBIC can be an existing company--or one that you can set up yourself. However it is involved, the SBIC lends your customers the funds they need on one condition: that you will step in and make good any loans on which they default. Once your customers have on hand the larger amount of working capital they can get by this means, they will be in a better position to make prompt payment to you for their purchases. You, in turn, will receive just that much more working capital to pump into the operation and expansion of your business; you will be able to reduce your accounts receivable, the funds needed to carry those receivables, and therefore your need to borrow funds. And there are tax advantages as well.

A Way to Build Customer Loyalty

The arrangement should appeal to your customers. Not only will you bolster their long-term financial health (and thus your own), but you will undoubtedly earn some gratitude for finding them financial aid--and that gratitude could well be translated into greater long-term customer loyalty. Finally, you will avoid the embarrassment of having to dun your customers for overdue payments while your salesmen are simultaneously trying to get new orders. Instead, an impersonal third party, the SBIC, will assume the responsibility of playing the "bad guy." And as most businessmen know, a loan collector, whether he is really a bad guy or not, generally stands a better chance than a supplier of getting paid on time.

In exploring the possibilities of such a setup, first check out existing SBICs, as listed in the Appendix: you might find one that is conveniently enough located, sufficiently capitalized, and familiar with businesses in your field. If you are unable to find one suited, or willing, to enter into such an agreement, you can form a new SBIC of your own.

Using an Established SBIC

Seeking the services of an SBIC that is well established and knowledgeable in financing, of course, will save you the worries of forming and operating a new company--a big consideration if you already have your hands full with your own business and hesitate to take on the management of a separate, unfamiliar financial enterprise. Sound out several likely looking SBICs and talk to your accountant and lawyer as well. When you find a company that appears to be a good prospect, draw up an agreement under which you will refer to the SBIC any customers who need financing and with whose credit you are generally satisfied, and under which you will guarantee to cover any of their unpaid loans.

Two Ways to Guarantee the Money

A guarantee agreement with an SBIC can take one of two basic forms:

• Direct guarantee. Your company agrees to take over the responsibility for, and to pay directly to the SBIC, any amount still due if one of your customers defaults on his loan, customarily secured by the goods you have shipped to him. Once you have paid off the SBIC, the rights to any such collateral revert from the SBIC to you.

• Indirect guarantee. Instead of assuming the responsibility for paying off a bad loan, you agree to swap for the bad loan, in its entirety, a good loan you already hold with another customer on your own. For example, you may have already extended a line of credit of $25,000 to Customer A long before you sought additional financing for other customers through an SBIC, and Customer A has been paying you regularly and on time. Under your arrangement with the SBIC, it has lent $25,000 to Customer B, who at first is prompt about his payments but then runs into problems and is forced to default on his loan. To satisfy the SBIC under the terms of your agreement, you simply exchange loans with it: you sign over Customer A's good loan to the SBIC, which collects the interest and remaining principal repayments on it; in turn, the SBIC hands over to you its bad loan to Customer B, on which you must now attempt to collect. Naturally, the good loan you substitute must be for at least as much as the amount of the bad loan. It can, of course, be for a larger amount of money, in which case the SBIC remits to you the excess portion of each payment of interest and principal it collects on the good loan.

It's Your Responsibility

Under either a direct or an indirect guarantee, if a customer defaults on a loan it becomes your responsibility, not the SBIC's, to try to recoup your investment; you will have to repossess your goods and attempt to sell them to other customers, assuming, of course, that the goods are not of a quickly perishable type and that they are still in good condition. (You should make sure that some of your employees know how to repossess property, or that you have expert professional repossessors lined up in your company's various sales regions, particularly in those that are located far afield.)

Since the SBIC, as a loan collector, is more likely to be paid on time than you might be as a supplier, it is probably a good idea not to broadcast knowledge of the guarantee agreement you have with the SBIC. If your customers were to find out, they might tend to treat the SBIC more like a supplier than a loan collector because of its relationship to you, and be more lax in their payments. A final word of caution: even though the loans make it possible for your customers to pay you regularly for their purchases, you should continue keeping a reserve for bad debts to cover your guarantees to the SBIC.

Using Your Own SBIC

In helping to finance their customers, quite a few companies have found it preferable to form their own privately held SBICs. Not only can such an arrangement be more economical in the long run; it also gives a company closer control over its dealings with its customers, and provides the owners with certain tax advantages, as explained in Chapter 7. The most immediate benefit a company realizes from owning its own SBIC is the leverage that the arrangement can provide for its own funds--leverage that gets its force from the fact that an SBIC can borrow from the Small Business Administration up to four times the amount of its invested private capital. Moreover, these loans from the SBA are obtained at the same advantageous interest rate as the federal government itself pays for long-term funds-- usually 2½ or more percentage points under the prime rate charged by banks.

Here's an example of how it can work. Your company has found it necessary to allot $500,000 of working capital to carrying its monthly accounts receivable. By forming your own SBIC and investing $500,000 in it as capital, you become eligible to borrow for your SBIC a great deal more working capital: up to four times that amount, or $2 million. Thus you could put together a total pool of as much as $2.5 million, if needed, to finance your customers, and because of their new ability to pay you promptly for their purchases you could also reduce the amount of working capital ordinarily tied up in accounts receivable. As your business and theirs expand, you could draw on the pool to finance increased sales to old customers, and to finance entirely new customers you would like to add to your list. Naturally, on such loans you will want to charge an interest rate at least as great as your own cost of money from the SBA, preferably enough more to cover the costs of operating your SBIC; even if you set this rate at 1 or 2 percentage points higher than your own cost of borrowing, your customers would probably still be getting a bargain compared with the going rate of most bank or finance company loans. If you do set up your own SBIC, you should transfer your reserves for bad debts, normally carried on your books as deductions from your accounts receivable, over to the SBIC in the form of reserves for its outstanding loans.

Success Stories

There are many examples of companies that have benefited from forming their own SBICs. One is Farm House Foods Corporation of Milwaukee, Wisconsin, an independent wholesaler of grocery products, which formed Bankit Financial Corporation so it could help finance present and future customers who operate retail grocery stores. Bankit, with a private capitalization of $350,000, can borrow up to $1.4 million in additional funds from the SBA. Its ability to provide financing for customers who need added cash is explained by Farm House salesmen as they make their rounds of grocery stores. To date Bankit has made loans varying in size from $10,000 to $70,000, the maximum amount it is permitted under SBA regulations, which limit loans to any one business to 20 percent of an SBIC's private capital. With the help of Bankit, Farm House Foods has not only increased its sales to existing customers but has taken on new customers attracted by the ready availability of funds.

Private SBICs have proved valuable in other fields as well. Tyler Refrigeration Capital Corporation, set up by Tyler Refrigeration of Michigan City, Indiana, helps finance Tyler distributors who sell the company's products to retail stores. Tyler's normal policy is to lend one dollar for every dollar of a distributor's own capital; if a particular distributor is short of equity, Tyler will provide additional funds, and take a small ownership position in the distributor's operation, by purchasing stock. Many holders of franchised retail chains also use their own SBICs. Meyers Dairy Products of Cleveland, Ohio, set up Tomlinson Capital Corporation to aid in the financing of its dairy and food mart franchisees, of which it now boasts nearly 100. One of the nation's largest fast food corporations, Burger King of Miami, Florida, has expanded its business into fresh territory by forming Burger King MESBIC, Inc., which assists minority entrepreneurs in obtaining franchises to own and operate their own local Burger Kings.

If you feel that your company might profit similarly by establishing its own small business investment company, the next chapter will tell you in detail how to set one up.

Chapter Seven

HOW TO FORM YOUR OWN SBIC

If you decide to finance your customers by means of your small business investment company, you will have to go about forming one along certain lines established by law. Though it does require both organization and paperwork--quite a bit, in fact--the formation of an SBIC is not difficult, particularly since the Small Business Administration stands ready to help. The more SBICs that are formed, the SBA reasons, the more private investors and lenders there will be to ensure the good health of small business without the need for direct government aid.

As outlined in Chapter 5, there are two types of small business investment companies that can be formed. The most common, known in government jargon as a Section 301(c) SBIC, is appropriate to the majority of business situations. The other, known as a Section 301(d) SBIC, MESBIC or Minority Enterprise SBIC, is essentially similar but is especially designed to assist small business entrepreneurs who belong to racial minority groups and/or are located in economically depressed areas.

If the majority of the customers whom you wish to finance are indeed disadvantaged as defined in the Act, you should form a MESBIC because of its advantages--compared to an SBIC--as a borrower from the SBA. Either an SBIC or a MESBIC can borrow up to 400 percent of invested capital from the SBA. An SBIC, however, borrows from the SBA at the same rate as the federal government pays when it borrows money. But a MESBIC has an even better deal; it may actually borrow up to twice its capital by selling the SBA cumulative preferred stock at 3 percent--cash in return for a bargain-basement interest rate; then, it may borrow the remaining 200 percent of its capital in the form of 10-year subordinated debentures. For the first five years the MESBIC pays at an interest rate that is 3 percent less than the government pays for its funds; for the last five years of its debentures it pays the same rate as the government pays.

What an SBIC Is, and What It May Do

Before starting to prepare a license application for an SBIC or MESBIC, you and your attorney would do well to read the Small Business Investment Act and the SBA rules and regulations designed to carry it out. Copies are available from any office of the SBA; the address of the office nearest you can be found in Appendix A of this book.

Broadly speaking, the Act defines an SBIC as a corporation, duly chartered or incorporated by appropriate state authorities, that is licensed by the SBA to conduct only those activities contemplated in the Act: the financing of small businesses by loans and/or equity investments, and

74

the rendering of expertise to such businesses in the form of consulting and/or management services.

Tax Advantages of an SBIC

As shareholder of an SBIC, there are a number of different tax advantages for you and/or your present company, as well as for other shareholders and for the SBIC itself.

A major inducement to investors contemplating an investment in an SBIC is the shareholder's right to treat gains on the sales of his stock in the SBIC as long-term capital gains, and to treat losses on his stock, arising from sale or exchange, as unlimited ordinary-loss deductions. This is in contrast to the normal tax treatment of such losses as capital losses as specified in Section 1242 of the Internal Revenue Code.

A substantial tax advantage of the SBIC itself is its right to treat gains and losses on the sale of stock holdings as capital gains and losses; moreover, it may treat losses on the sale of convertible debentures, or on stock received from converting a convertible debenture to stock, as unlimited ordinary-loss deductions. If it were not for this special tax treatment, both kinds of losses would have to be treated as capital losses under Section 1243 of the Internal Revenue Code.

The Internal Revenue Service has also exempted any SBIC from the usual surtax on accumulated profits, provided the SBIC is actively engaged in providing financing to small business concerns. Thus, in contrast to an ordinary company, an SBIC can continue to accumulate its profits and avoid the surtax for doing so, normally imposed under the Regulation 1.553-1(d) of the Internal Revenue Code.

In addition, in the case of an SBIC, the Internal Revenue Service has waived the usual definition of a personal holding company and the tax imposed thereon, provided no shareholder of the SBIC owns, directly or indirectly, 5 percent or more of a business in which the SBIC invests. Normally, the IRS generally looks for two conditions in defining a personal holding company: (a) 60 percent or more of its ordinary income derives form passive sources such as dividends, interest, and rents; and (b) more than 50 percent of its outstanding stock is owned by five or fewer individuals at any time during the last half of the taxable year (Section 542, IRC).

Other special tax benefits for an SBIC:

• It may deduct from its earnings a full 100 percent of dividends received from the investments it makes in taxable small businesses, instead of the 85 percent deduction allowed other corporate taxpayers for dividends received (Section 243, IRC).

• An SBIC is permitted to carry back net operating losses for 10 years instead of the usual three years; it is permitted to carry forward net operating losses for seven years, just as ordinary companies can (Section 172, IRC).

• SBICs are allowed to establish bad debt reserves for loans made to the small business companies in their portfolios. Having such a reserve gives the SBIC a tax advantage not available to many businesses that have to justify establishing bad debt reserves; the SBIC can take part of what would be its pretax earnings and put it in the reserve, reducing taxable income and taxes, but not cash flow. The amount of such a reserve is based, for any SBIC, upon actual loss experience for the current year and the five preceding taxable years, but if the SBIC is less than six years old it is based on the average loss of companies in the SBIC industry--currently about 5 percent of the total of the average SBIC's outstanding loans (Section 586, IRC).

• An SBIC that is publicly owned and registered under the Investment Act of 1940 can, like mutual funds and other investment companies, "pass through" its earnings to shareholders and thus avoid the payment of a corporate income tax on these earnings. To do this, however, the SBIC must derive at least 90 percent of its gross income from dividends, interest, and gains from the sale of stock; it must distribute to its shareholders not less than 90 percent of its net income, excluding income from capital gains; and it must be diversified like any other publicly owned financial institution in its investments and loans (Section 851(b) and (c), IRC). Ordinarily, an SBIC--whether publicly or privately owned--can pay dividends from earnings only after corporate taxes have been paid on its earnings.

A similar right to "pass through" earnings, as well as tax deduction for losses, has been granted to an SBIC established as a limited partnership, a special type of SBIC authorized by an amendment to the SBA act made in 1977. The general partner of such an SBIC must be a sole corporate partner as defined by law; the limited partners may add directly to their individual incomes and their pro-rata shares of the profits of the SBIC, paying ordinary income tax on them; they may also deduct directly from their individual incomes their pro-rata share of any losses of the SBIC. Thus a limited partnership can "pass through" to its limited partners both income and losses without either of these being subjected to corporate taxation (or deduction).

Since the rights, liabilities, and tax advantages of any limited partnership can vary widely depending on how it is set up, you should consult a lawyer and/or accountant with some knowledge in this specialized field. In fact, a competent lawyer and accountant will be of immeasurable help in showing how any of the above tax advantages may apply in an individual case, as well as in assisting you to draw up your application to the SBA for any SBIC.

Preparing an Application

An application to form an SBIC, which is filed under Section 107.102 of the SBA regulations, consists of two main elements, an SBA form 415 entitled "Small Business Administration License Application," and an SBA form 415A entitled "Statement of Personal History and Qualification of Management," as well as various exhibits that accompany the forms. Forms and exhibits for the main application, 415, must be made in triplicate and sent, along with a license-processing fee of $500 (nonreturnable even if the application is denied) to the Small Business Administration, 1441 L Street NW, Washington, DC 20416.

In order to help applicants, a sample application and accompanying exhibits for an imaginary SBIC appear in Appendix C on page 194. Both application and exhibits were prepared from SBA-supplied materials and actual SBIC applications, and are intended for use as a guide.

All exhibits--they actually constitute the bulk of the application-- should be typed on good quality bond paper (the required duplicates and triplicate may be either carbon copies or photocopies as long as they can be clearly read). Each exhibit must be identified at the top by (1) a number reference to the related item, (2) the name of the license applicant, (3) the caption designated for such item, and (4) the date of submission. Separate sheets must be used for each exhibit; if more than one sheet is necessary for an exhibit, the sheets must be stapled together at the top.

In making out your application, you should bear in mind certain requirements set down by the SBA:

• Name approval. The name of your new SBIC must be okayed by the SBA as well as by the incorporating state authority, and cannot make use of misleading and suggestive words like "United States," "National," "Federal," "Reserve," "Bank," "Government," or "Development"; moreover, it should not be so similar to that of another organization as to imply association with that organization unless permission is obtained (see application Item 1).

• A bona fide office. Your SBIC cannot be run "out of your hat": it must have its own office space even if that space is only one room in the offices of another business entity--where you display your license, maintain a publicly listed telephone, are open to the public during normal business hours, and show the SBIC's name on a building directory or street-level sign (Item 2).

• Minimum capital. The company must be capitalized with at least $500,000 of private capital exclusive of organizational expenses; this must be shown on the application either pro forma (as planned) or as the actual total capital (paid-in capital and paid-in surplus) as of a particular date (Item 3). The accompanying exhibit on capitalization should also briefly describe different classes of stock, voting rights, and all provisions relating to dividends, liquidation, preemption, conversion, redemption, and assessments and/or limitations on disposition.

You must also describe how the capital has been, or is to be, raised (Item 4), either by public stock offering or private sale (including in the latter case the number and names of persons buying stock, their relationship to you, and whether they are taking the securities for investment or for resale to others). You must describe the manner of the offering-- whether it is personal contact, use of printed sales literature, news- papers, paid salesmen, or a combination.

• Corporate owners. If a corporation will own 10 percent or more of the voting securities, you should state the number of owners of the equity securities of that corporation, and what percentage of the corporation's total assets are being invested in your SBIC.

• Geography is important. The SBA requires that you describe the main geographical area in which your SBIC plans to operate (Item 5), but in order not to restrict your area of future operations it is wise to add "and in other areas of the United States, its territories and possessions as may from time to time be approved by the SBA," and to append "without regard to the location of any small business with which it-deals."

• Financing needs. You are also asked to describe the need for the type of financing to be supplied by your SBIC in its operating area (Item 6). The SBA assumes from experience that there are not enough sources of capital in most areas for the adequate financing of small business con- cerns. Nevertheless, you should describe specific difficulties in your area, relating to the particular types of businesses you intend to fi- nance, and attach copies of any pertinent articles that have appeared recently in newspapers, magazines, business reviews, or bank newsletters.

• Loans or equity? Under your Plan of Operations (Item 7), start off with "broad policy" wording stating that you as the applicant recogize the need of small businesses for both equities and loans; this is not only in the spirit of the Act but allows you maximum flexibility in any future activities of your SBIC. Under this umbrella, state whether you plan to emphasize loans or equity investments, what management consulting services you intend to offer (business consulting, appraising, feasibility reports, placement of institutional loans, etc.), and whether or not you intend to use an investment adviser. If any officer, manager, or 10 percent owner of your SBIC has any affiliation with any other SBIC licensee or his investment adviser, you must describe it, as well as any affiliation that may exist between an investment adviser you decide to use and any officer, director, or manager of your proposed SBIC. If you are applying to form a MESBIC, you must also pledge to make investments only in disadvantaged minority enterprises, and to guarantee that the parent company will pay initial operating costs of the MESBIC if its capitalization is small.

• Owners, officers, and managers. In describing the Management and Control of your SBIC (Item 8--see Sections 107.101(a) and 107.702 of the SBA regulations) you should list, in clear tabular form, the names, addresses, and titles of all officers, directors, general managers, investment advisers, and owners of 10 percent or more of your SBIC's voting stock, their annual rates of compensation and other emoluments, and what percentage of each class of capital stock or other securities of your SBIC each will own. (The majority of your directors, and the majority of your officers and managers, must be U.S. citizens.) If one of your 10 percent owners is a corporation, give the names and addresses of all beneficial holders of

81

10 percent or more of the voting securities of that corporation, and the percentage owned by each. If you have a contract with any of the above persons or corporations, you must submit a copy of it as part of the exhibit. If any of your shares are to be owned, directly or indirectly, by anyone else, or are to be transferred to be resold, made subject to loans, or subject to any understanding as to voting rights, you must also state the details. If you sell preferred stock in your SBIC, you cannot redeem it except under certain safeguards specified in SBA regulations.

• Certified articles of incorporation. As part of your application, you must provide a copy of your SBIC's articles of incorporation certified by the appropriate authority of the state in which it is incorporated (Item 9). The articles must state that the corporation is "organized and chartered solely for the purposes of operating under the Small Business Investment Act of 1958, as amended," and they must adhere not only to the laws of the state but to certain other provisos of the SBA relating to powers and responsibilities of the SBIC as stated in the Act and accompanying regulations. You are also required to submit certified copies of the proposed bylaws of your SBIC, which should follow the form acceptable in the state of incorporation (Item 10); certified copies of the minutes of the corporate meeting at which the directors were elected (Item 11); certified copies of the minutes of the meeting of directors at which the corporate officers were elected (Item 12); and certified copies of the resolution of the board of directors authorizing the execution and filing of the license application (Item 13).

• Banks and deposits. You must submit as an exhibit a brief statement giving the name of the bank (or banks) in which your SBIC plans to deposit

82

its cash, and the name of the bank (or banks) your SBIC plans to name as custodian of its securities (Item 14). You should also ask the bank to address a letter to the SBA stating how much of your SBIC's cash and/or securities it is holding, giving the account numbers and spelling out any encumbrances or restrictions against such deposits (Item 15). You may deposit funds in an interest-bearing escrow account, such as a savings account, and need not formally invest them in your SBIC until the SBA notifies you that it plans to approve your license application. You will receive sufficient warning to make the transfer of funds from the escrow account to the SBIC's account.

• SEC clearance. Before the SBA will issue a license, it must have evidence from the Securities & Exchange Commission that any securities issued by your SBIC meet SEC requirements (Item 16). SEC clearance is not required if the SBIC is to be 100 percent owned by a corporation and the value of all the SBIC's securities to be owned by the corporation does not exceed 5 percent of the corporation's total assets. Nor is clearance required if it is otherwise readily apparent that the applicant is not subject to the registration provision of the Securities Act of 1933 or the Investment Company Act of 1940. In either one of these circumstances, you only need to have an independent counsel--not your own lawyer--submit his opinion that your SBIC is automatically exempt.

• Lawyer's statement to the SEC. In a letter to the Securities & Exchange Commission (500 North Capitol St., Washington, DC 20549), your lawyer should furnish the following information: (1) The number of shares to be issued and their par value; (2) the total number of persons or organizations offered the stock, and the number of actual investors to date; (3)

how the stock was offered (approached through personal contact not involving paid salesmen, sales literature, or advertising); (4) any intention to offer additional stock in the future; (5) the names of anyone holding 10 percent or more of the voting stock (and if such a holder is a corporation, whether the value of the securities is 5 percent or more of the corporation's total assets); (6) whether or not the applicant is asking for an exemption from the registration provision of the Securities Act of 1933 (Section 4(2)) and/or the Investment Company Act of 1940 (Section 3(c)(1)).

• Compliance with the law. Your legal counsel is also required to submit a written opinion to the SBA stating that you have complied with all applicable local, state, and federal laws in the formation of your SBIC; that you have followed the applicable regulations and laws in the sale of stock; that your SBIC is properly chartered to conduct only the activities described in the Small Business Investment Act; and that it is properly authorized and entitled to conduct these activities upon issuance of a license (Item 17).

You must list as a separate exhibit the names and addresses of your legal counsel, accountant, and anyone else who helped you prepare your license application, as well as a description of the services rendered and the amounts of the fees paid (Item 18).

• Final declaration. To complete the corporate application, Form 415, you are required to submit a declaration (Item 19) that you will operate your SBIC in conformity with the Act and SBA regulations; that you will not improperly use any funds of the SBIC or engage in transactions that involve conflicts of interest as defined in SBA regulations; and that all the information submitted in your application and exhibits is true and correct. The declaration must be signed by the applicant and by all officers and shareholders owning 10 percent or more of the SBIC's stock.

Personal History Forms

To make sure the managements of SBICs are qualified to operate efficiently and responsibly, the SBA also requires each officer, director, general manager, and owner of 10 percent or more of voting stock to file a statement of his or her personal history and qualifications to manage (Form 415A). If any 10 percent owner is a corporation or other entity, forms must be filed by each stockholder or owner of that corporation whose individual share of ownership in the SBIC would amount to 10 percent or more. In addition, the corporation must submit as an exhibit a copy of its own balance sheet as of a reasonably recent date.

Form 415A is a fairly straightforward request for business and personal information. Among other things, it asks for a summary of business experience over the last 10 years, a description of education and degrees received, three character references, and "yes" and "no" answers to various questions directed at the answerer's personal and business probity. Copies of the form are obtainable through any office of the SBA. Sometimes the SBA may also require personal interviews with members of its Washington staff.

Public Notice and Publication

Once the SBA receives your license application, it is required by law to publish a notice of the application in the Federal Register, giving the name and location of the proposed licensee firm, its areas of operation, and the names and addresses of its officers, directors, general manager, and owners of 10 percent or more of its voting stock. The notice must provide any interested parties the opportunity to submit written comments to the SBA about the application and any of the information given.

You, as the applicant for the license, are also required to publish such a notice in a newspaper of general circulation in the city, area, or areas in which you intend to operate. You must furnish the SBA with a certified copy of this notice within 10 days after it has been published.

Getting Help with Your Application

Before submitting a final license application to the SBA, you would be wise to discuss a working draft of it with someone in the office of SBIC Operations in the Washington headquarters of the Small Business Administration.

If you need additional information, or advice derived from the experiences of other SBICs, contact Walter B. Stults, Executive Vice President of the National Association of Small Business Investment Companies, 618 Washington Building, Washington, DC 20005 (202-638-3411).

Chapter Eight

SPECIAL
FEDERAL PROGRAMS

Although the U.S. Government helps American businessmen largely
through the Small Business Administration and its licensed SBICs, financial aid for particular situations is also available from other federal
sources. The Department of Housing and Urban Development, for example, in-
sures mortgage loans for builders of housing and renewal projects; the
Maritime Administration promotes the construction of merchant vessels;
the Overseas Private Investment Corporation encourages companies to do
business with friendly developing nations by making loans or guaranteeing
their investments abroad. The whole spectrum of government loans, guarantees, research and demonstration grants, and other aids to organizations
and individuals, business and otherwise--some 1,078 programs administered by 57 different agencies--is detailed in a remarkable 2-inch-thick
document called the Catalog of Federal Domestic Assistance, available

annually for $20 from the U.S. Government Printing Office, Washington, DC 20402. Whether you are looking to finance a new business in the energy field, or to send a college graduate to Europe on a Fulbright scholarship, there may be something in it for you.

Of broadest interest to many businessmen, next to SBA's own offerings, are three major programs aimed at promoting healthy regional economies. These are administered, respectively, by the Farmers Home Administration of the Department of Agriculture, by the Department of Commerce's Economic Development Administration, and by various regional commissions such as those set up to deal with the particular problems of Appalachia, the Ozarks, New England, and the Upper Great Lakes. All are authorized to help businesses, directly or indirectly, to enter or operate in areas of the U.S. that are relatively poor or undeveloped--for reasons that may include competition from cheap imported goods.

Help from the FmHA

The largest of the three programs (in terms of dollars) is the Farmers Home Administration, which deals with a far larger population than that represented by farmers. In one recent year, the agency guaranteed private business loans worth more than $1 billion. Over many years, the FmHA has, of course, helped individual farmers with loans for farm operation, irrigation, soil and water conservation, flood prevention, and family housing; it has also become increasingly interested in aiding business and industry to improve the economic climate in rural communities by raising employment and income there. The 1,500-plus business loans it guaranteed last year ranged from $11,000 to $33 million, with an average of about $900,000.

Among the smaller amounts were $32,000 to enable an employee of a neighborhood grocery store to buy and continue to operate the business, $115,000 to set up a dental practice in a small town, and $150,000 to obtain a franchise for a McDonald's fast-food restaurant. In the middle range, a truck stop operator obtained $600,000 to expand his motel and restaurant; a bottler of mineral water got $980,000 to renovate; and a furniture company received $2.5 million to build a steam heating plant utilizing its waste wood scraps for fuel. At the high end, the FmHA guaranteed a $16.7 million loan to Robin International Corp. of Greenville, Mississippi, to build a rice-processing factory; the record $33 million went to American Cotton Growers of Littlefield, Texas, to build a cotton denim mill supplying blue jean fabric to Levi Strauss & Co.

A Preference for Small Towns

Loans under FmHA's business and industrial programs are guaranteed only for companies located in towns having a population of 50,000 or less and in suburban areas where the population density is no more than 100 persons per square mile. Preference is given to applicants in rural areas and towns with populations of 25,000 or less. Loans may be for business or industrial acquisitions; construction, conversion, or modernization of plant and equipment; purchase of land, buildings, or machinery; start-up expenses and working capital; waste disposal facilities or pollution abatement and control. The FmHA normally requires that the lender be a local institution that routinely provides credit to firms and individuals in the area.

The maximum loan that the FmHA will guarantee is based on a formula governed by the number of jobs (at $10,000 per job) that the loan will help a company to save or create for the area's economy. The maturity of a loan may run up to a maximum of 30 years for land, buildings, and permanent fixtures (or their useful lives, if shorter); the maximum maturity for a loan for machinery and equipment is 15 years and for working capital, seven years. Interest rates are determined by negotiations between the lender and borrower. However, since the federal government guarantees most of the loan-- up to 90 percent, with 10 percent or more of equity required from the applicant--the interest rate is likely to compare favorably with what the lender charges its better credit risks. The FmHA, for its part, charges the lender a one-time guarantee fee of 1 percent of the guaranteed amount (e.g., $900 of a $100,000 loan that is 90 percent guaranteed) and this fee may be passed on to the borrower as part of the cost of obtaining the loan. The borrower must also pledge any and all available collateral to protect both FmHA and the lender from default. This may consist of the borrower's accounts receivable, machinery and equipment, first or second mortgage, or a personal guarantee. The integrity and ability of management, the soundness of the project, and the prospect of earnings are all considered in determining the collateral required. And in the rare event that a normal lending institution cannot be found to make the loan, the FmHA itself may agree to make a loan, basing its interest rates on the government's own cost of borrowing.

The Ground Rules

As with all government-backed loans, certain restrictions apply.

- The company receiving the loan must be 51 percent or more owned by

U.S. citizens or permanent legal residents.

 • The money cannot be used to finance a project that might result in the transfer of business and employment out of the area or that is likely to produce more goods or services than the area demands.

 • The loan cannot be used to finance a transfer of ownership unless this will keep the business from closing or cutting back on its number of jobs.

 • The money cannot be used to guarantee lease payments, or to make payments to stockholders or partners who retain ownership in the business or to any other government agency from which the company may have a loan outstanding.

 • The borrower must comply with standard federal regulations such as those regarding equal employment opportunities, clean air and water, and historic site preservation.

How to Investigate and Apply

To look into the possibility of an FmHA-guaranteed loan, contact the FmHA county supervisor in your area; for his number, check the local telephone book under U.S. Government, Department of Agriculture, Farmers Home Administration. If there is no listing, get in touch with the state office of the FmHA (Appendix F). Normally the county supervisor will review your case and pass it along to a district director, who will forward it to the state director for action. If the loan application is for $1 million or more, it is generally sent to Washington for final approval or rejection. The usual time required is 90 to 120 days in all, so it is wise to start well ahead of the time when you will actually need the cash.

In addition to guaranteeing direct private loans to individual businesses, the Farmers Home Administration makes industrial development grants to local public agencies--village, township, county, and state authorities--to acquire and develop land and buildings for rural industrial sites. How to investigate possible advantages to your own business under this program is explained in Chapter 9.

Financial Assistance from the EDA

To encourage long-term growth in economically backward or distressed areas, whether rural or urban, the Department of Commerce's Economic Development Administration has three major programs to assist businesses that are unable to raise funds by conventional means. Under its Business Development Assistance Program, EDA makes direct loans to finance the cost of land, building, and equipment to provide working capital; it also guarantees up to 90 percent of loans made by private lenders for these purposes and up to 90 percent of rental payments on leased buildings, equipment, and land. To be eligible, a company must be establishing a new business, or expanding an old one, in a designated EDA redevelopment area; a list of such areas, updated quarterly, is available from the EDA director in your region (Appendix E). Designated areas are generally those with high unemployment, low median income, or a history of sudden vacillation in the availability of jobs. An application for assistance must meet EDA's overall goals for the area in question and must be approved by the town, county, or other political subdivision concerned; moreover, the borrower must demonstrate that the money is not available from normal sources on reasonable terms.

Borrowing to Buy Assets

Direct loans for the acquisition of fixed assets are made by the EDA up to 65 percent of costs, including land, land preparation, buildings, machinery, and any engineering and legal fees. Of the remaining 35 percent, the applicant must put up 15 percent in equity capital or a subordinated loan, and a bank or other lending institution takes a first mortgage on the first 20 percent. The loan, like those of FmHA, is limited to a maximum of $10,000 per job that will be saved or created for the region; the smallest loan is generally $500,000 and the average is $1 million. Maturity is a maximum of 25 years or the life of the fixed assets, whichever is shorter; interest rates are based on the government's own cost of borrowing, usually well below the bank prime rate. Collateral in the form of a second mortgage to the EDA or a personal guarantee may be required.

Direct loans for as much as 100 percent of needed working capital may also be made by the EDA, even though the agency normally requires that a company's assets exceed its liabilities by 15 percent at the time the loan is made. The minimum loan is usually $500,000, based on the formula of $10,000 per job saved or created; the maturity is five to 10 years and the interest rate is the same the government pays. As collateral, accounts receivable and inventory must be pledged.

Backing for Private Lenders

The EDA will also guarantee loans negotiated by you with private lenders, working on the same formula of $10,000 per job. On a guaranteed loan for fixed assets the applicant must put up 15 percent of the costs. The EDA will then guarantee up to 90 percent of the remaining 85 percent advanced by the bank. Loans may run up to a maximum of 25 years, or the life of the fixed assets. The EDA will also guarantee up to 90 percent of a loan made by a bank for working capital needs, provided that assets exceed liabilities by 15 percent; loans may run five to 10 years and, like the others, are based on the formula of $10,000 per job. The agency may also guarantee up to 90 percent of your rental payments on land, buildings, and machinery if you do not own them, up to a lease of five years and sometimes more.

Among recent recipients of EDA assistance are the Genbearco Company, which obtained a $1.2 million direct loan to build a new ball-bearing plant in Wilson, North Carolina, and thereby create more than 150 new jobs; Virginia Products Corporation, which received $2.1 million to construct a factory producing aluminum windows and doors that eventually will bring nearly 500 jobs to its area; Pueblo Wire and Tube of Colorado, which got a $500,000 bank loan, guaranteed by EDA, as working capital to boost its production and increase its work force; and Viewflex Audio-Visual of Holbrook, New York, which received a direct $750,000 working capital loan that is expected to preserve 114 existing jobs and create 61 more.

Protection from Imports

Under legislation passed in 1974, the EDA is authorized to assist companies, and communities, that have been adversely affected by increased competition from cheaply manufactured goods imported from overseas. On successfully demonstrating to the agency that its sales and/or work force have suffered for a period of three years, a company may receive technical or financial aid. Technical assistance in developing an adjustment plan can be provided either by a federal agency or by a private institution such as a management consulting firm; in the latter case, EDA will pay up to 75 percent of the cost.

Financial aid may be in the form of direct loans up to $1 million, which can be used by a company to expand, improve, or automate its plant, or to branch out into a totally unrelated field that will guarantee its employees jobs. In addition to--or in place of--a direct loan, the EDA will guarantee up to 90 percent of a loan made by a private lender, with a ceiling of $3 million. Loans for fixed assets have a maximum maturity of 25 years; loans for working capital run five to 10 years. In 1978 technical assistance was extended to 89 firms and financial aid to 70, many of them footwear manufacturers feeling the pinch of rising imports from low-salary nations like Korea and Taiwan. The budget for the program has been rapidly increasing, nearly doubling in each of the last two years to reach a recent total of $96 million.

EDA's Special Assistance Program

Through another program, the Economic Development Administration indirectly aids businesses in regions threatened with economic deterioration due to the loss of a major employer, or a sucession of smaller employers, whether that loss is due to relocation, depletion of natural resources, compliance with environmental regulations, the closing of a military installation, or some other cause. Under this program--officially titled the Special Economic Development and Adjustment Assitance Program--Long-Term Economic Deterioration (LTED)--EDA makes an initial grant of $25,000 to $150,000 to a state, county, town, or other local agency to study the problem and prepare a counterstrategy. Then it follows up with implementation grants of anywhere from $250,000 to $5 million to help the agency carry its strategy out. This money, in turn, serves as a pool from which the local agency can make loans to individual companies for working capital, technical assistance, training, and other purposes that will eventually help the region as a whole.

Saving Thousands of Jobs

For example, when the Fibreboard Corporation announced plans to close its plants at Stockton, California, and Portland, Oregon, the EDA granted $5.5 million to California's San Joaquin County to help save the 1,200 jobs involved. The county used the funds to make a long-term, low-interest loan to a stock ownership trust formed by Fibreboard employees; the trust, in turn, formed a new company, Pacific Paperboard Products, to purchase the assets of the two plants and operate them. More than 900 jobs at Stockton and 300 at Portland were saved and the economies of both areas avoided a heavy blow.

Similarly, when Rockwell International proposed to close a building-hardware factory in Morgantown, West Virginia, EDA granted $4.7 million to the state, which extended a loan to a newly formed company, Sterling Faucet Co., to buy out Rockwell and maintain the plant's 800 jobs. Anticipating expansion of the Redwood National Park in Humboldt County, California, and the consequent loss of lumbering and sawmill jobs due to forest land being closed to cutting, a newly formed Redwood Regional Economic Development Commission obtained a $5.5 million EDA grant; with the money it established a revolving loan fund to help other businesses in the area expand, thus creating new jobs and taking up the slack. When the Queen Mine in

Brisbee, Arizona, ran out of ore to extract, the community got EDA funds to loan to the company, which opened up a new lode--tourism. Today, safety-helmeted sightseers ride through the Queen on narrow-gauge rail cars, enjoying a new experience and bolstering the town's economy by spending their dollars at the mine and at local motels, restaurants, and stores.

In exploring the possibility of EDA aid under any of the above programs, you should first contact the EDA office in your region. An EDA representative will be assigned to review your request and help you with the necessary staff conferences and forms. In your application, you must demonstrate the capability and experience of your management, including resumes of officers and key employees and personal financial statements if collateral is to include a personal guarantee. You will also have to provide data on markets and competition, proposed use of funds, start-up costs, projections of cash flow, raw materials, and other information normally required for a conventional loan. Applications for new ventures requesting more than $1 million, and any projects involving tourism, must be accompanied by feasibility studies prepared by qualified independent consultants. An environmental impact statement may also be required.

How Regional Commissions May Help

Finally, your company may stand to benefit, directly or indirectly, from federal-state partnership in public development projects if it operates in certain areas of the U.S. for which special regional commissions have been set up. One of these is the Appalachian Regional Commission, which awards project grants to public bodies and non-profit agencies in West Virginia and parts of 12 other states grouped along the Appalachian mountain chain from Alabama to New York.

In addition to building needed highways and access roads, one of the commission's objectives is to bring new industry into areas subject to the boom-and-bust cycles of coal mining, as well as to rehabilitate land damaged by strip-mining practices. Other goals are to encourage development of low and moderate income housing, health care and child development programs and facilities, job training centers, and various other projects. These range from local arts and crafts programs to timber development, the disposal of junk cars, and various solid waste and energy-related enterprises.

Similar long-range economic development plans involving state-federal partnerships are administered by the Coastal Plains Commission, covering designated counties in North and South Carolina, Georgia, Florida, and Virginia (grants for model solar homes, the design of port facilities for the seafood industry, sewer and water extensions to serve major tourist attractions, and industrial sites); the Four Corners Regional Commission, concerned with development in Arizona, New Mexico, Colorado, Utah, and Nevada (an alternative energy program producing methane from agricultural wastes, development of domestic rubber from the guayule plant, and high-grade lubricants from the jojoba bean); the New England Regional Commission, covering the six New England states (railroad rehabilitation, demonstration projects to encourage conservation and the development of new energy sources and thus reduce the region's dependence on oil); the Ozarks Regional Commission, including Arkansas, Kansas, Louisiana, Missouri, and Oklahoma (industrial sites, satellite hospitals, technical education centers, water and sewage treatment plants, access roads and railroad spurs); the Upper Great Lakes Regional Commission, covering parts of Michigan, Minnesota, and Wisconsin (industrial development, transportation, tourism, and recreation); and the Old West Regional Commission, including Montana, Nebraska, North and South Dakota, and Wyoming (improved agricultural production, and a computer-based farm management system, industrial development, recreation, tourism).

For further sources of information on any of these programs, and for referral to the appropriate agency, you can make inquiries at either your state department of commerce or state economic development agency, which should be well aware of both the federal and state financial assistance programs.

Preparation and the Personal Touch

Though the paperwork and procedures involved in securing government aid can be complex and time-consuming, you can speed the process by careful preparation, and by talking to the right person at the right time. A telephone call to the appropriate local official, followed by a personal visit, will usually yield more helpful, understandable information and establish a better rapport than an exchange of formal letters. In most cases there will probably be more applications to a given agency than there are funds available. You may well be able to improve your chances for approval by seeking out introductions and endorsements of your project at as many political levels as possible as your applications moves upward through the levels of government. Don't hesitate to enlist the aid of local politicians. You, your company, and your employees are important to the economic health of your community and the civil servants representing it, and through family relationships every individual in your business represents three or four votes--or more. A politician will realize this fact of life more sensitively than you do, and his influence may be able to make the difference in getting the financing that you need.

Chapter Nine

BORROWING THROUGH STATE AND LOCAL GOVERNMENT AGENCIES

In all 50 states, you have a choice of literally thousands of aid agencies in smaller political subdivisions--counties, cities, and towns that make financial assistance available to companies within their boundaries. Their motives are not purely altruistic, of course: new jobs and a healthier economy are the prizes for any community or region that can attract new business, or hold onto existing business and encourage it to expand. And in competing with each other for attention, some communities and regions have developed attractive inducements indeed.

Waiting May Be Worth It

As with other forms of government-aided financing, borrowing through a state or local agency is no free ride: it requires both paperwork and patience. Obtaining needed funds can take anywhere from two to six months, and sometimes more. It may also take some investigation to find the right people to talk to at the right time so as to speed things along. But for businessmen, especially those having trouble raising money by more conventional means, the wait can be well worthwhile.

As a group, state and local agencies are far too numerous and varied to list or describe in individual detail. You can find out about those in your region easily enough by asking around in the business community, particularly among bankers and Chamber of Commerce officials.

Or, you may go directly to the agencies themselves. Look in the telephone book under the name of your state (e.g., "Nebraska"): there you will probably find a listing such as "(Nebraska) State Development Agency" or "(Nebraska) Industrial Development Agency" or "(Nebraska) Economic Development Administration." If not, look under "(Nebraska) Commerce Department" or "Department of Commerce"; the department may administer business assistance programs itself or, if not, can refer you to the specific agency that does. Similarly, you can look in the book under the name of your county, city, or town for a local agency that has "development," "industrial," and/or "economic" in its name. A telephone call will probably yield the initial information you need, some descriptive literature, and an appointment for a follow-up interview.

Examples in the Empire State

The various possibilities of aid available in states and local communities are clearly visible in the State of New York. As one of the more populous states, New York has developed a broad range of programs for helping business and industry. The state government has a number of major agen-

102

cies, whose names describe their roles: the Urban Development Corporation, the Job Development Authority, the Business Development Corporation, the Environmental Facilities Corporation, and the Business Marketing Corporation. Beyond these, at last count, counties and municipalities around the state boasted a total of no less than 115 local development corporations, or LDCs, and 129 industrial development agencies, or IDAs. This array of public and quasi-public bodies offers a broad spectrum of financial aid to business in the form of tax incentives and low-cost building, machinery, and equipment loans.

New York's Urban Development Corporation is perhaps best known for large-scale projects like New York City's $375 million Convention and Exhibit Center, a $100 million hotel conversion, and a $50 million headquarters for the American Stock Exchange. But it has also helped finance a $10.8 million plant for Sybrom Corporation in Rochester and a $5.5 million one for Carborundum Corp. in Niagara Falls, a $4.5 million Sheraton Hotel in Utica, a $2.5 million Lazzaroni Bakery in Ramapo, and a $600,000 facility for the Brockport Cold Storage Co. in Brockport. To encourage projects it deems desirable, UDC floats tax-exempt bond issues and uses the proceeds to offer companies various financing plans, buying the real estate and equipment necessary and leasing them back to the companies for a specified period, or guaranteeing loans by conventional lenders. It also uses staff specialists and consultants--planners, architects, engineers, financial analysts, lawyers--to offer technical help when needed.

Loans Make Jobs

A case in point in New York is the Job Development Authority, which was established to aid business in creating and retaining job opportunities in the state. To accomplish this, the JDA makes low-cost, long-term second mortgage loans for the construction of new manufacturing plants and research facilities, for the acquisition and rehabilitation of existing industrial buildings, for the purchase of machinery and equipment, and for the installation of pollution controls. It will make direct loans of up to 40 percent of a project's total cost, with a loan ceiling of $1 million; it will also guarantee loans by others to a maximum of 80 percent of the cost or $1 million. To raise funds to support its efforts it sells bonds that are exempt from federal taxes (the reason it must limit its participation to $1 million under IRS Code). The authority will also help out with a second mortgage to supplement a bank's first mortgage, provided the bank's mortgage does not exceed 50 percent of the project's cost.

A Pool for Lending Risks

The New York Business Development Corporation makes smaller loans of $25,000 to $500,000 on five- to 10-year terms to companies that are unable to qualify as good credit risks for conventional loans (most states have similar agencies). Rather than having to lend directly to such companies, banks and other lenders can pool their risks by lending instead to the Business Development Corporation, which in turn advances funds to the companies under normal collateral requirements and at standard bank-interest rates. A loan is serviced by a conventional lender, usually the company's regular bank. The BDC charges a modest filing fee of $75, plus an additional $1 per $1,000 of the loan's amount.

In addition to loans, the BDC makes equity funds available through a

wholly owned subsidiary, licensed by the federal Small Business Administration as an SBIC. From smaller companies, this SBIC will purchase convertible debentures or subordinate notes with terms of five to 10 years, or
common or preferred stock up to a maximum of $60,000 though larger amounts
can be arranged if other SBICs participate.

Ecological Aid

To help firms meet environmental standards set by the federal government, the state, or municipalities themselves, New York offers aid through
the Environmental Facilities Corporation. It issues special tax-exempt
revenue bonds so that companies can build or improve facilities for air
pollution control, water management, resource recovery, or disposal of
solid wastes.

Free Advice

The Business Marketing Corporation was established specifically to
attract business to New York City and help keep it there. A private, non-
profit organization funded through the city's Office of Economic Development, it does not make loans but instead furnishes a wide range of marketing
and counseling services without charge. BMC performs research and analy-
ses on investment and job development possiblities, outlines possible tax
credits and abatements, helps with site selection, warehousing and distribution planning, and supplies information on costs of materials,
labor, energy, and insurance. It also presents interested companies with
studies on the general cost of living and the city's overall attractions as
a place to live. To help the BMC in its counseling efforts, New York City

businesses, labor unions, civic organizations, and the city itself lend the services of experts on their staffs.

Public Benefit Corporations

Other cities, towns, and counties around New York have also set up their own organizations to lure new business firms and assist older ones to remain and expand. The most numerous are the 100-odd industrial development agencies, or IDAs, created in cities and towns as public-benefit corporations under the state's municipal laws. An IDA may issue tax-exempt revenue bonds and use the money to purchase mortgages on new or existing buildings, equipment, and machinery needed by companies it wishes to attract. The agency leases such facilities to the companies and uses the rents received to pay the principal and interest on the bonds. When a bond has been paid off in full and retired, the property is sold to the company for a token sum.

During the period of its lease, the company enjoys several advantages. It can take the depreciation and investment tax credits allowable on the buildings and equipment, even though it does not own them, and it can carry the debt outstanding on the bond as a liability on its books. The interest rate, negotiated between the company and the IDA, is substantially lower and the time period much longer than for conventional loans. Moreover, construction materials used on the project are exempt from the state mortgage tax. A company pays no real estate taxes while it is leasing its facilities from the IDA, assuming this burden only after the lease has expired and it takes over ownership (in some cases companies are asked to make payments in lieu of taxes, but usually at a lower rate than the normal prop-

106

erty tax). An IDA can issue up to $10 million in tax-exempt bonds for any one company over a six-year period; there is no dollar ceiling on facilities for pollution control.

Companies that have recently taken advantage of IDA financing in New York include National Cash Register, whose new plant in Albany was constructed with the help of $710,000 in tax-exempt bonds issued by the Albany County Industrial Development Agency, and Ahlstrom Machinery, Inc., which built a new factory with $1.5 million advanced by the IDA in the city of Glens Falls.

Similar to industrial development agencies, but operating usually in smaller communities and dealing in projects of lesser size, are the 100-odd local development corporations that have been established around New York State. Aimed at reducing unemployment and improving the quality of life in their areas, they are authorized to borrow money, issue tax-exempt bonds and other obligations, and to buy, sell, mortgage, and lease real estate. They can assist businesses to build new office quarters or acquire and remodel older space; they can also provide aid in residential development and rehabilitation.

Setting Up on Your Own

An agency like a local development corporation or an industrial development agency can be established in New York--or almost anywhere else--by citizens concerned with ensuring their community's health. Though precise laws differ from state to state, generally the incorporators must file a certificate of incorporation as a non-profit organization in the state capital, outlining their purposes and the public or quasi-public objectives to be achieved. If no such body exists in the area where your business is located or plans to locate, it may be worth your while to look into setting one up.

Chapter Ten

GOING PUBLIC – OR PRIVATE

Selling shares in your company in the form of stocks or bonds, either to the public at large or to selected institutional investors, is a time-honored method of raising capital. It is one of the main sources of financing for large and successful corporations, but it can be utilized by smaller, growing firms as well. In addition to the thousands of companies whose securities are publicly traded on various exchanges around the country, there are thousands more that have sold shares to private buyers. These are generally institutions such as investment companies, insurance companies, pension funds, foundations, and college endowments.

How Do Others See You?

Whether you decide on a public offering or a private placement of your securities--or wind up rejecting both in favor of some other form of financing--will depend on the nature of your company and, even more importantly, on how others see it, which may be quite different from the way you do. First of all, investors must be interested in the industry in which you operate. Second, they will want to know how well you have done compared with others in the industry, and what your projects for the future are. Third, more knowledgeable investors will take a close look at your operating practices. For example, you may have been in the habit of undervaluing your inventory or expensing certain items (like improvements to machinery) that might better be capitalized; likewise, you might be carrying a greater reserve for bad debts than is actually necessary. While such practices are sound and acceptable to you and your accountant, they will result in lower earnings; as a result, your company may seem less attractive to investors.

Talking to the Experts

The first step in making the decision is for you and your financial officer to talk to people familiar with the money market: your banker or bankers, financial consultants, securities underwriters who float public offerings, agents who handle private placements of stocks and debt. In these discussions you will want to bear in mind the three basic types of securities: common stock, preferred stock, and debt, which includes various kinds of debentures and bonds. Buyers of common stock, the basic form of ownership in a company, have much to gain if the stock appreciates in value, but they also have the least protection in the event the company runs into hard times. Preferred stock, which may or may not have any rights to ownership, comes ahead of common stock on claims to be paid off. Holders of debt have no ownership rights but have the greatest protection. They are the first to be paid if financial difficulties arise.

Because of the time and expense involved, a public offering seldom makes sense for a company that needs only a moderate amount of financing, say $1 million or less. But for a firm that is looking for more than a million, or several million, dollars, there can be some definite advantages-- particularly if that firm is in an industry popularly thought of as a "hot" investment, and particularly if its sales and earnings show a greater growth potential than competitors in its field. Over the past several years, growth industries favored by the investing public have included many in the so-called high-technology area--electronics, computer products, solar energy--as well as other growth areas such as oil and gas exploration, health care, gambling, and mail-order merchandise. Recent public issues of this kind have included ones of relatively modest size: General Hydrocarbons, Inc. (oil and gas exploration, $1.2 million); Health Extension Services (home health care, $750,000); Optelecom, Inc. (electro-optic products, $1.1 million); and Shopsmith, Inc. (power woodworking tools, $2.7 million). Larger ones includes Computer Devices, Inc. (desktop computer terminals, $4.2 million); L. Luria & Son (catalogue merchandise, $4.6 million); Ramtek Corp. (computer graphic displays, $5.3 million); and EDO Corp. (electronic equipment, $5.7 million).

The Public Move

A company that needs added capital, and feels confident enough to go public for it, can derive many advantages from such a move. In the very process of placing its securities on the market it generates publicity for itself. Its products or services become better known, not only to potential investors but also to prospective customers and suppliers. Some of these may themselves become shareholders, acquiring an additional interest in furthering the company's welfare by buying--or supplying components or materials for--the company's products.

By going public, a company obtains a rating for its securities through an agency like Moody's or Standard & Poor's. Ratings, in turn, help securities analysts evaluate the company and recommend it to their investing clients; as more people buy the company's stock the value of the stock and the company's reputation grow, making it easier for the company to obtain additional financing through another stock issue at a later date.

A publicly held company is able to attract and hold outstanding executives by offering them options in its stock, which they can sell to realize substantial capital gains that are taxable at a lower rate than the income they receive from their regular salaries.

A publicly held company with tradeable securities achieves added flexibility in the marketplace. It can issue new shares in order to make future acquisitions of other companies without having to part with needed cash, or it can sell new issues to raise cash needed for working capital or other purposes. Conversely, if a company finds itself in a surplus cash position, it can repurchase its own securities on the open market if it feels they are undervalued, waiting until their price-earnings ratio improves, when it can resell them if desired; or it can buy its own stock back in order to head off a takeover by an outside party or parties and to assure greater

112

control over its destiny.

Going public, of course, has some disadvantages. The process can be a long and demanding one for a company's senior executives, requiring perhaps five months between the initial decision to study the possibility, through approval by the federal government's Securities & Exchange Commission, to the moment when the stocks or bonds are finally sold (see table, page 126). It is also expensive, involving considerable outlays for lawyers and accountants, in addition to payment to an underwriter of a "discount" or "spread" between the market price of the stocks or bonds and the amount the company actually receives for them. In some typical recent transactions, for example, the underwriters' spreads averaged around 10 percent for companies making public offerings of $2.5 million or less, or as much as $250,000. On top of that, the companies' own expenses connected with preparing the offerings averaged another 4 percent, or up to $100,000, with some ranging as high as 8 percent.

Continuing Costs

Moreover, after its securities have been sold a company continues to bear added administrative expenses, including the preparation, printing, and mailing of annual reports and proxy statements to shareholders and the filing of periodic reports with the SEC. Fees must also be paid to agents for issuing dividend or interest payments and for registering and transferring stock. If the public comes to value the company's securities at many times their book value, which often happens, the estate tax evaluation on the holdings of its principals may be much higher than if the company had remained privately held.

Cards on the Table

Once the stock is on the open market, too, a firm can no longer play all its cards close to the vest: SEC regulations require that proprietary information--sales, profits, salaries, fringe benefits, and, often most importantly, technical data and methods of operation--be made available to the public, which includes the company's competitors. The actions of its executives are subject to scrutiny and criticism by the SEC, by shareholders, and by the press; not everyone may approve of various company decisions (on executive compensation, for example), and questions may arise about the potential impact of its operations on the communities in which it does business or on the environment as a whole. And not a few businessmen have made the bitter discovery that once a company is publicly held it can also be taken over by anyone who has accumulated enough of its shares, or who makes a tender offer to acquire the majority of the outstanding shares.

Planning and Professional Advice

Since the risks as well as the rewards are high, a public securities offering should be planned carefully and as far as possible in advance. The main responsibility should be at the top--retained by you or given to your company's chief financial officer, whatever his title may be. He, in turn, should enlist the aid of an accountant familiar with stock offerings and a lawyer experienced in securities law. In addition, both he and other executives of the firm should seek the advice of outsiders who have had experience with public offerings, including businessmen, bankers, and officials of the nearest regional office of the Securities & Exchange Commission (the SEC's 17 regional offices and their chiefs are listed in Appendix G on page 226).

Selecting an Underwriter

The opinions and suggestions of all these sources can be of substantial help in the next, crucial step: selecting the right underwriting firm--or syndicate of firms, in the case of a larger offering--through which your securities will be sold. Look closely into the track record of several such firms: the types and sizes of their most recent public offerings; the types and sizes of the companies for which such offerings were made; the feelings of such companies about how the underwriters handled the job; the performance of the securities themselves after the initial issue; and what kind of support the underwriters gave them, such as keeping the public abreast of the company's doings after the issue had been on the market for a while.

Bear in mind that an underwriter does not work on a fee or commission basis in the usual sense; he is actually a principal in a business transaction who buys your company's securities from you and offers them to the public at a higher price, using the spread between the two figures to cover his own profit and costs. The price at which an underwriter buys your securities can be determined either by negotiation or by competitive bidding. In a negotiated sale, the company and the underwriter reach a mutually acceptable figure; for an issue that appears to be easily salable, the spread should be less than for one that will require a lot of work. If you consider a proposed spread great enough to be questionable, you can see if another underwriter may be willing to do it for less and still provide the same services and support.

Bidding Breeds a Higher Price

In a competitive sale, the price paid to a company for its securities is generally the highest that the winning bidder thinks he can pay and still market the securities at a profit, and is therefore usually higher than a negotiated price. It is also easier to arrive at, since the underwriters automatically establish the price in the bidding process. On the other hand, it is more expensive and time-consuming to deal with several underwriters instead of one. Besides, the time schedule for a competitively bid offering is less flexible than for a negotiated offering; the pricing must be set much earlier by each bidder before you can decide which one you will be working with, and this can be a disadvantage in a stock market that is moving either up or down. Also, there is always some danger that an offering price that is set too high as an outcome of competitive bidding may result in a poor reception for the securities on the part of the buying public. It may also set a weak after-market price that may take a long period of time to correct.

Filling in the SEC

Once agreement is reached with an underwriter, a registration statement describing the offering must be prepared for filing with SEC headquarters in Washington, D.C. This chore, carried out by your lawyers and the underwriter's lawyers working together, can take a good month. The SEC charges a registration fee that is computed at 1/50 of 1 percent of the total offering (e.g., $2,000 on a $10 million investment), with a $100 minimum.

The SEC is not concerned with judging the relative merits of your offering in the marketplace; it is charged by law with making sure that the securities are not offered to the public under cover of misleading information, and that all true and relevant information about the offering, and your company, is properly disclosed (any unusual risk factors in the company's business, or a higher-than-normal underwriter's compensation, for example, must be revealed up front in the registration statement). Beyond this, the SEC will keep an eye on the contents of your company's annual reports and proxy statements, and any suspicious trading of company stock by "insiders" such as chief executives or directors; it is also charged with the supervision of brokers' dealings with their customers and the overall operations of the stock exchanges.

Another month and a half may elapse while SEC officials review your statement, raise questions, and ask that certain amendments be made before giving their go-ahead. There are no shortcuts in this process, but there can also be unexpected dividends: by forcing you to take a hard look at your own company, both the professional financiers and the government regulators may help you to discover hidden weaknesses in your operation whose correction could turn out to be of considerable long-term value to you and the company.

Red Herrings and Prospectuses

When the registration statement seems likely to be approved, you and your underwriter may want to generate some advance interest by distributing a preliminary prospectus that describes the offering to potential buyers; such a document is often referred to as a "red herring" because it must bear a prominent legend, usually printed in red ink, advising the reader that a registration has been filed but that the securities cannot actually be offered for sale before the date the registration is approved. When a registration does become effective, a final prospectus--the legal document offering the securities for sale--is printed and distributed to potential buyers, including those who received the preliminary one. The stock certificates or bonds themselves must also be designed and printed prior to any sales being made.

Total costs for printing a red herring, prospectus, and certificates can come to $40,000 to $55,000 for an average-sized offering of $5 million. Other costs will include the expense of an audit by your accounting firm, which can range from $10,000 to $40,000 or more, depending on the size of the company; legal costs of $25,000 to $90,000; and from $20,000 to $30,000 for a liability insurance policy to protect you and the underwriter from possible lawsuits charging that you failed to disclose full and proper information about the offering to the public. In addition to these direct expenses, there may be substantial indirect expenses, principally the time of company officers and staff diverted from their normal duties to deal with the preparation of the offering over a period of five months or more.

When the securities have finally been offered for sale, a closing is scheduled at which the company receives the proceeds: the gross amount the underwriter expects to receive from the sale minus his compensation, which covers his profit, his overhead, his own legal and accounting expenses, and his commissions to salesmen and discounts to participating dealers.

A somewhat simpler procedure can be followed for smaller public offerings under Regulation A of the Securities Act, which exempts a company from filing a registration with the SEC if its offerings do not exceed a total of $1.5 million in any one year; to this figure may be added the sale of any shares of the company already held by you or other individual shareholders, provided they do not exceed $100,000 per shareholder or $300,000 for three or more shareholders.

So-called "Reg A" offerings are processed by regional SEC offices rather than the Washington headquarters, take about half as much time as large-scale offerings to prepare and get approved, and cost about a third as much. Although an offering circular must be supplied to prospective buyers, it need not be as lengthy or detailed as a formal prospectus; a "red herring" is also permitted as long as the company is using an underwriter for the offering.

Most larger underwriters, being geared to larger offerings, are reluctant to take on Reg A issues, but smaller firms often will (it is important to check their credentials and track records closely, as not all small underwriters are as reputable as most larger ones). A company can act as its own underwriter and salesman on a small offering, as it can on a larger one provided it has determined in advance that there is a definite market for its securities and it knows precisely how to proceed. (Getting into any securities offering without professional help adds to the risks and can well result in not finding enough buyers to make the issue successful.)

The Private Placement

Though public offerings of stocks and bonds are best known to the general public, many more companies in recent years have been raising capital by selling their securities to private institutional investors. A private placement, in fact, may be the only workable alternative in your case. Many professional underwriters, as we have noted, will not consider handling a public offering unless it is large enough to be worth the time and money. Even if the offering contemplated is large enough to attract an underwriter and the company is well-enough known to appeal to a sufficient number of buyers, an uncertain or downward-trending market may make a public offering inadvisable.

If the company decides it does not wish a public offering, but still needs funds for any reason, it would do well to consider a private placement of securities, either with investment companies, insurance firms, or the managers of pension funds or other funds held in trust. A private placement, since it does not involve the general public, need not be registered with the SEC.

Though the difference between a "public" and a "private" offering has never been precisely defined as a point of law, an offering is usually considered private if no more than 25 potential purchasers are offered a chance to buy the securities in question. If the purchasers buy in amounts greater than $150,000 each, there is no limit on the number of purchasers.

Professionals and Long-Term Investors

In any case, however, they must be experienced professional buyers-- institutions with trained staffs able to obtain on their own, without the protection of a prospectus, all the information they need on which to base a sound decision whether to buy or not to buy. They must also purchase the securities with the intent of holding them as investments; if they intend at the time of purchase to resell for a profit they are considered underwri-

120

ters according to law. This does not mean that a buyer cannot ever resell your securities, only that he must have held them for a reasonable period of time prior to resale.

Time and Cost Savings

A private offering of securities has many advantages over a public one. To begin with, it takes about half as long to consummate--eight to 10 weeks, on the average, compared with four or five months. Expenses are substantially less because a private placement involves far lower accounting and legal fees and printing costs.

A private placement has other advantages. Terms can be adjusted during discussions with private investors to allow for special situations: irregular income projections, and provisions for additional purchases by the buyers at some future date (in a public offering these would be impossible, since prospective buyers cannot be approached without a written prospectus and since all discussions must be restricted to the terms contained therein). A private offering also allows a company greater flexibility in modifying or delaying its sale of securities without having to change and resubmit material filed with the SEC; it can even call off the sale if it has to without suffering the costly results that canceling a public offering would entail.

An Agreed-on Price

Private placements, moreover, are sold at a firm price agreed on in advance. This is in contrast to a public offering, in which the market price of the securities may change during the time it takes to arrange the offering and sell the shares. Changes in the terms after a private placement can also be negotiated at a later date; the company need deal only with a small number of known purchasers. Because they have bought for the long term and wish to protect their investment, they are more likely to talk new terms than to move against the company if a provision of the agreement should go into default. By developing close relationships with the buyers of its securities, a company assures itself of sources that could prove increasingly valuable as it grows and needs additional funds. Last, and far from least, by making a private offering rather than going public a company avoids having to broadcast disclosures of sensitive information on its sales, earnings, and salaries--not to mention trade secrets on which its corporate life and future may depend.

On the reverse side of the coin, a private placement does have a few disadvantages. It must be limited to a small number of experienced institutional buyers; it cannot include anyone who happens to walk in off the street with some spare cash to put to work. Compared to the terms of a public offering, private placements are usually more restrictive as to the company's minimum working capital and maximum long-term debt.

The price an experienced buyer will agree to for a given security is also likely to be less than what an inexperienced investor might be willing to pay; he is well aware of the savings a company can realize through private financing and expects to share in them. And privately offered securities receive no Moody's or Standard & Poor's ratings, which restricts their being considered by many large institutions, and no market exists from which the company can repurchase its own securities.

An agent's fee in a private placement is appreciably less than the usual underwriter's spread. For placements in the $1.5 million range, for example, an agent will charge a fee of about 1 to 1.5 percent, or $15,000 to $22,500; on its own expenses in connection with the placement, a company can expect to pay an additional 1.5 to 3 percent, or $22,500 to $45,000. For placements in the neighborhood of $5 million, agents' fees range from .5 to .75 percent, or roughly $25,000 to $37,500, with company expenses coming to an added .7 to 1.5 percent, or $35,000 to $75,000. In the $15 million bracket, the fees drop to .37 to .5 percent, or $55,000 to $75,000; company expenses should amount to about .4 to .6 percent, or $60,000 to $90,000. If you can time your private placement within 90 days of the end of your fiscal year, you may be able to save yourself $20,000 or more in accounting expenses by using your regular year-end audit to show to prospective buyers rather than commissioning a special one; the lower percentages for company expenses given above are predicated on this economical move. Unless you or your company financial officer have already had some experience with private placements, and can spare the time out from the daily operation of your business, you should not attempt one without using some kind of agent or consultant.

A qualified agent may be a knowledgeable member of an investment banking firm, financial consulting firm, or a commercial bank, or he may be an independent specialist in private placements working on his own. An increasing number of prospective purchasers welcome their services, too, because they know that an experienced agent will bring to them only placements of the type and size they are interested in, and will save them precious time by making sure those placements are properly structured and prepared before being shown.

A good agent or financial consultant can be invaluable in advising a company whether to consider a private placement versus a public offering-- or, for that matter, whether the company's particular situation is better suited to some other form of financing such as borrowing from a finance company, factoring, or restructuring its existing debt with banks. If a private placement is decided on, the agent can indicate to you how current conditions in the money market might affect the sale, tell you which potential buyers have funds to invest and which are fully committed, and advise you on what criteria various investors follow as to minimum and maximum amounts and the types of companies in which they are wiling to invest. An agent can help you decide on the type, timing, and price of the placement and can aid in preparing the necessary memorandum or offering circular, tailoring it to the particular investor or investors who will be approach- ed (in contrast to printing and distributing a full prospectus for a public offering, the few needed copies of the circular and accompanying financial statements can simply be run off on an office duplicating machine).

Smoothing the Rough Spots

In dealings with prospective buyers, the agent can assist in negoti- ating terms and reviewing documents, and he can act as a middle man to smooth things out should disagreements arise. If necessary, he can make a discreet "no-name canvass" of potential buyers, describing the securities to be offered and the type of industry in which the company operates without actually divulging the company's name. In this respect a skilled agent will take care to avoid too much obvious "shopping around." Prospective buyers do not like to spend a lot of time investigating an issue only to find

124

they may not have an opportunity to buy it, nor do they like to go on record with prices that may be used against them as a means of bargaining with other prospective buyers. If a rumor spreads in the financial community that an issue has been "shopped," investors may conclude there is something wrong with the seller because no one seems to want what he has to sell.

With the guidance of a good agent, a private placement should move along on a schedule resembling the one shown in the table on page 128, requiring two months or so from the time the company's directors approve the idea to the time the securities are sold. For simplicity's sake the sample schedule is given starting with the beginning of the calendar year, but you may be able to save considerable accounting costs by timing a placement to coincide with your regular audit toward the end of your fiscal year.

Schedule for a Public Offering

Highlights of a typical schedule (the initial date of January 1 has been chosen arbitrarily as a base from which to count the time required for each step).

Date	Action	Responsibility
Jan. 1-31	Company decides to study public offering as a means of raising funds.	Company president and financial officer.
Feb. 1	Company recommends plan to board of directors; directors approve issue.	Company president, financial officer, and board of directors.
Feb. 2	Underwriters notified of issue being authorized by board.	Financial officer
Feb. 28	Tentative agreement by company with underwriters or group of underwriters.	Officers of company and underwriters.
Mar. 1-15	Assembly and preparation of material needed for registration statement.	Officers and employees, counsel, accountants for company.
Mar. 16-25	Preparation of registration statement.	Counsels for company and underwriters.

Mar. 26-31	Registration statement printed.	Printer and counsels for company and under- writers.
Apr. 1	Registration statement filed with SEC in Washington, D.C.	Company counsel.
Apr. 2-30	SEC letters of comments discussed and appropriate amendments to registration made.	Company and under- writers' counsels.
May 15	Registration statement declared effective by SEC.	SEC
	Agreement signed by underwriters with company.	Officers of company and underwriters.
	Securities offered for sale by underwriters and dealers.	Salesmen of under- writers and dealers.
May 22	Closing between underwriters and company, which receives proceeds less underwriters' compensation.	Officers and counsel for company and underwriters.

Schedule for a Private Placement

Date	Subject	Responsibility
Jan. 1-21	Company decides to study private placement as means of raising funds.	Company president and Financial Officer
Jan. 22	Company recommends plan to Board of Directors and Directors approve placement.	Company President, Financial Officer and Board of Directors
Jan. 23	Potential buyers such as institutions notified of placement being authorized by Board.	Financial Officer
Jan. 23-Feb. 7	Assembly and preparation of material needed for offering circular.	Officers and Employees, Counsel, Accountants
Feb. 8-14	Preparation of offering circular.	Officers and Employees
Mar. 7	Tentative agreement by Company with buyer or group of buyers.	President and Financial Officer
Mar. 8-31	Preparation of legal documents required by buyer.	Officers and Counsels of Company and Buyer
Apr. 1	Closing between Company and buyers.	Officers and Counsel of Company and Buyer

APPENDIX A

U.S. SMALL BUSINESS ADMINISTRATION

Region		Address and Telephone
I	Boston, MA 02110	60 Batterymarch St., 10th floor, (617) 223-2100
	Boston, MA 02114	150 Causeway St., 10th floor, (617) 223-2100
	Holyoke, MA 01050	302 High St., 4th floor, (413) 536-8770
	Augusta, ME 04330	*40 Western Ave., Rm. 512, (207) 622-6171
	Concord, NH 03301	*55 Pleasant St., Rm. 211, (603) 224-4041
	Hartford, CT 06103	One Financial Plaza, (203) 244-3600
	Montpelier, VT 05602	*87 State St., Rm. 204, P.O. Box 605, (802) 229-0538
	Providence, RI 02903	57 Eddy St., 7th floor, (401) 528-4580
II	New York, NY 10007	*26 Federal Plaza, Rm. 29-118, (212) 264-7772
	New York, NY 10007	*26 Federal Plaza, Rm. 3100, (212) 264-4355
	Melville, NY 11747	401 Broad Hollow Rd., Suite 322, (516) 752-1626
	Hato Rey, PR 00918	*Chardon and Bolivia Sts., P.O. Box 1915, (809) 753-4572
	St. Thomas, VI 00801	*Veterans Dr., Rm. 283, (809) 774-8530
	Newark, NJ 07102	*970 Broad St., Rm. 1635, (201) 645-2434
	Camden, NJ 08104	1800 E. Davis St., (609) 757-5183
	Syracuse, NY 13260	*100 So. Clinton St., Rm. 1071, (315) 423-5383
	Buffalo, NY 14202	*111 W. Huron St., Rm. 1311, (716) 846-4301
	Elmira, NY 14901	180 State St., Rm. 412, (607) 733-4686
	Albany, NY 12210	99 Washington Ave., Rm. 301-Mezzanine, (518) 472-6300
	Rochester, NY 14614	*100 State St., Rm. 601, (716) 263-6700
III	Philadelphia, Bala Cynwyd, PA 19004	231 St. Asaphs Rd., Suite 646-West Lobby, (215) 597-3311
	Philadelphia, Bala Cynwyd, PA 19004	231 St. Asaphs Rd., Suite 400-East Lobby, (215) 597-3311
	Harrisburg, PA 17101	100 Chestnut St., 3rd floor, (717) 782-3840
	Wilkes-Barre, PA 18702	20 No. Pennslyvania Ave., (717) 826-6497
	Wilmington, DE 19801	*844 King St., Rm. 5207, (302) 573-6294
	Baltimore, Towson, MD 21204	8600 LaSalle Rd., Rm. 630, (301) 962-4392
	Clarksburg, WV 26301	109 No. 3rd St., Rm. 301, (304) 623-5631
	Charleston, WV 25301	Charleston National Plaza, Suite 628, (304) 343-6181
	Pittsburgh, PA 15222	*1000 Liberty Ave., Rm. 1401, (412) 644-2780
	Richmond, VA 23240	*400 No. 8th St., Rm. 3015, P.O. Box 10126, (804) 782-2617
	Washington, DC 20417	1030 15th St. NW, Suite 250, (202) 655-4000
IV	Atlanta, GA 30309	1375 Peachtree St. NE, 5th floor, (404) 881-4943
	Atlanta, GA 30309	1720 Peachtree St. NW, 6th floor, (404) 881-4325
	Birmingham, AL 35205	908 So. 20th St., Rm. 202, (205) 254-1344
	Charlotte, NC 28202	230 So. Tryon St., Suite 700, (704) 371-6111
	Greenville, NC 27834	*215 So. Evans St., Rm. 206, (919) 752-3798
	Columbia, SC 29201	*1835 Assembly St., 3rd floor, (803) 765-5376
	Jackson, MS 39201	*100 W. Capitol St., Suite 322, (601) 969-4371
	Biloxi, MS 39530	111 Fred Haise Blvd., 2nd floor, (601) 435-3676
	Jacksonville, FL 32202	*400 W. Bay St., Rm. 261, P.O. Box 35067, (904) 791-3782
	Louisville, KY 40201	*600 Federal Plaza, Rm. 188, P.O. Box 3517, (502) 582-5971
	Miami, Coral Gables, FL 33134	2222 Ponce De Leon Blvd., 5th floor, (305) 350-5521
	Tampa, FL 33602	700 Twiggs St., Suite 607, (813) 228-2594
	Nashville, TN 37219	404 James Robertson Pkwy, Suite 1012, (615) 251-5881
	Knoxville, TN 37902	502 So. Gay St., Rm. 307, (615) 637-9300
	Memphis, TN 38103	*167 No. Main St., Rm. 211, (901) 521-3588
	West Palm Beach, FL 33402	*701 Clematis St., Rm. 229, (305) 659-7533
V	Chicago, IL 60604	*219 So. Dearborn St., Rm. 838, (312) 353-0355
	Chicago, IL 60604	*219 So. Dearborn St., Rm. 437, (312) 353-4528
	Springfield, IL 62701	1 North, Old State Capital Plaza, (217) 525-4416
	Cleveland, OH 44199	*1240 E. 9th St., Rm. 317, (216) 522-4180
	Columbus, OH 43215	*85 Marconi Blvd., (614) 469-6860

```
        Cincinnati, OH 45202        *550 Main St., Rm. 5028, (513) 684-2814
        Detroit, MI 48226          *477 Michigan Ave., (313) 226-6075
        Marquette, MI 49855         540 W. Kaye Ave., (906) 225-1108
        Indianapolis, IN 46204     *575 No. Pennsylvania St., Rm. 552, (317) 269-7272
        Madison, WI 53703           212 E. Washington Ave., Rm. 213, (608) 264-5261
        Milwaukee, WI 53202        *517 E. Wisconsin Ave., Rm. 246, (414) 291-3941
        Eau Claire, WI 54701       *500 So. Barstow St., Rm. B9AA, (715) 834-9012
        Minneapolis, MN 55402       12 So. 6th St., (612) 725-2362


VI      Dallas, TX 75235            1720 Regal Row, Rm. 230, (214) 767-7643
        Dallas, TX 75242           *1100 Commerce St., Rm. 3C36, (214) 767-0605
        Marshall, TX 75670         *100 So. Washington St., Rm. G-12, (214) 935-5257
        Albuquerque, NM 87110       5000 Marble Ave. NE, Rm. 320, (505) 766-3430
        Houston, TX 77002           500 Dallas St., (713) 226-4341
        Little Rock, AR 72201       611 Gaines St., Suite 900, (501) 378-5871
        Lubbock, TX 79401          *1205 Texas Ave., Rm. 712, (806) 762-7466
        El Paso, TX 79902           4100 Rio Bravo, Suite 300, (915) 543-7586
        Lower Rio Grande Valley
          Harlingen, TX 78550       222 E. Van Buren St., P.O. Box 2567, (512) 423-4534
        Corpus Christi, TX 78408    3105 Leopard St., P.O. Box 9253, (512) 888-3331
        New Orleans, LA 70113       1001 Howard Ave., 17th floor, (504) 589-6685
        Shreveport, LA 71101       *500 Fannin St., Rm. 5B06, (318) 226-5196
        Oklahoma City, OK 73102    *200 NW 5th St., Suite 670, (405) 231-4301
        Tulsa, OK 74119             616 So. Boston St., (918) 581-7462
        San Antonio, TX 78206      *727 E. Durango St., Rm. A-513, (512) 229-6250
        Austin, TX 78701           *300 E. 8th St., (512) 397-5288


VII     Kansas City, MO 64106       911 Walnut St., 23rd floor, (816) 374-5288
        Kansas City, MO 64106       1150 Grande Ave., 5th floor, (816) 374-3416
        Des Moines, IA 50309       *210 Walnut St., Rm. 749, (515) 284-4422
        Omaha, NB 68102             19th & Farnum Sts., 2nd floor, (402) 221-4691
        St. Louis, MO 63101         1 Mercantile Center, Suite 2500, (314) 425-4191
        Wichita, KS 67202           110 E. Waterman St., (316) 267-6571


VII     Kansas City, MO 64106       911 Walnut St., 23rd floor, (816) 374-5288
        Kansas City, MO 64106       1150 Grande Ave., 5th floor, (816) 374-3416
        Des Moines, IA 50309       *210 Walnut St., Rm. 749, (515) 284-4422
        Omaha, NB 68102             19th & Farnum Sts., 2nd floor, (402) 221-4691
        St. Louis, MO 63101         1 Mercantile Center, Suite 2500, (314) 425-4191
        Wichita, KS 67202           110 E. Waterman St., (316) 267-6571


VIII    Denver, CO 80202            1405 Curtis St., 22nd floor, (303) 837-5763
        Denver, CO 80202            721 19th St., (303) 837-2607
        Caspar, WY 82602           *100 E. B St., Rm. 4001, P.O. Box 2839, (307) 265-5266
        Fargo, ND 58108            *657 2nd Ave., No., Rm. 218, P.O. Box 3086, (701) 237-5771
        Helena, MT 59601           *301 So. Park Ave., Rm. 528, Drawer 10054, (406) 449-5381
        Salt Lake City, UT 84138   *125 So. State St., Rm. 2237, (314) 425-5800
        Sioux Falls, SD 57102       101 So. Main Ave., Suite 101, (605) 336-2980
        Rapid City, SD 57701       *515 9th St., Rm. 246, (605) 343-5074


IX      San Francisco, CA 94102    *450 Golden Gate Ave., P.O. Box 36044, (415) 556-7487
        San Francisco, CA 94105     211 Main St., 4th floor, (415) 556-7490
        Oakland, CA 94612          *1515 Clay St., (415) 273-7790
        Fresno, CA 93712            1229 N St., P.O. Box 828, (209) 487-5189
        Sacramento, CA 95825       *2800 Cottage Way, Rm. 2535, (916) 484-4726
        Las Vegas, NV 89101        *301 E. Stewart, P.O. Box 7525, Downtown Sta., (702) 385-6611
        Reno, NV 89505             *50 So. Virginia St., Rm. 308, P.O. Box 3216, (702) 784-5268
        Honolulu, HI 96850         *300 Ala Moana, Rm. 2213, P.O. Box 50207, †(808) 546-8950
        Agana, GU 96910             Pacific Daily News Bldg., Rm. 508, †(671) 477-8420
```

130

Los Angeles, CA 90071	350 S. Figueroa St., 6th floor, (213) 688-2956
Phoenix, AZ 85012	3030 No. Central Ave., Suite 1201, (602) 261-3611
Tucson, AZ 85715	*301 W. Congress St., Rm. 3V, (602) 625-1063
San Diego, CA 92188	*880 Front St., Rm. 4-S-29, (714) 293-5440

X	Seattle, WA 98104	710 2nd Ave., 5th floor, (206) 442-5676
	Seattle, WA 98174	*915 2nd Ave., Rm. 1744, (206) 442-5534
	Anchorage, AK 99501	1016 W. 6th Ave., Suite 200, †(907) 271-4022
	Fairbanks, AK 99701	*101 12th Ave., Box 14, †(907) 452-1951
	Boise, ID 83701	1005 Main St., 2nd floor, (208) 384-1096
	Portland, OR 97204	*1220 S.W. 3rd Ave., Rm. 676, (503) 221-2682
	Spokane, WA 99210	*W. 920 Riverside Ave., Rm. 651, P.O. Box 2167, (509) 456-5310

*Federally owned properties. (All others federally leased.)
†Operator assistance may be needed in some areas.

SBA REGIONAL OFFICES — INVESTMENT STAFF

Region I   Connecticut, Massachusetts, Maine, New Jersey, New Hampshire, Rhode Island, Vermont, District of Columbia

| William W. Leopold | Chief | (202) 653-6930 |
| Robert Hull | Financial Analyst | |

Region II   New York, Puerto Rico, Virgin Islands

| Lawrence F. Friess | Chief | (202) 653-6427 |
| L. Victor Seested | Financial Analyst | |

Regions III & IV   Alabama, Delaware, Florida, Georgia, Kentucky, Maryland, Mississippi, North Carolina, Pennsylvania, South Carolina, Tennessee, Virginia, West Virginia

| Anthony DiMuzio | Chief | (202) 653-6473 |
| Milton A. Ganas | Financial Analyst | |

Regions V & VIII   Colorado, Illinois, Indiana, Michigan, Minnesota, Montana, North Dakota, Ohio, South Dakota, Utah, Wisconsin, Wyoming, Washington

| Jerome Dillon | Chief | (202) 653-6690 |
| Ronald H. Ward | Financial Analyst | |

Regions VI & VII   Arkansas, Iowa, Kansas, Louisiana, Missouri, Nebraska, New Mexico, Oklahoma, Texas

| Richard Pippel | Chief | (202) 653-6926 |
| William P. Delaney | Financial Analyst | |

Regions IX & X   Alaska, Arizona, California, Guam, Hawaii, Idaho, Nevada, Oregon

| Marvin D. Klapp | Chief | (202) 653-6935 |
| Douglas H. Burch | Financial Analyst | |

APPENDIX B

DIRECTORY OF SMALL BUSINESS INVESTMENT COMPANIES

Following is a listing by state of all operating SBICs (Part I) and Minority Enterprise SBICs (Part II) licensed by the U.S. Small Business Administration to lend to or invest in businesses whose individual net worth does not exceed $6 million and whose after-tax earnings do not exceed $2 million. All may qualify to supplement their private capital by taking out long-term loans from the SBA in an amount not to exceed four times their private capital.

KEY

Under the column headed "Investment Policy," the following group definitions for SBICs are identified by the numbers at left:

15. Building Construction, General Contractors and Operative Builders

16. Construction other than Building Construction--General Contractor

26. Paper and Allied Products

35. Machinery except Electrical

36. Electrical and Electronic Machinery Equipment and Supplies

38. Measuring, Analyzing, and Controlling Instruments; Photographic, Medical, and Optical Goods; and Watches and Clocks

70. Hotels, Rooming Houses, Camps, and other Lodging Places

*Code Number	Type of Ownership
1	Bank dominated (50% or more owned by bank or bank holding company)
2	Bank associated (10% to 49% owned by bank or bank holding company)
3	Financial organization other than bank or bank holding company (public or non-public)
4	Non-financial organization (public or non-public)
5	Individually owned (privately held)
6	Investment company (1940 Act)
P	After code number signifies partnership

PART I: OPERATING SBICs BY STATE

LICENSEE	INVESTMENT POLICY	OWNER CODE
ALABAMA		
Benson Investment Company, Inc. William T. Benson, President 406 South Commerce St. Geneva, Alabama 36340 (205) 684-2824	Diversified	5
Coastal Capital Company Chris C. Delaney, Suite B Mobile, Alabama 36606 (205) 432-0064	Builders	3
First SBICI of Alabama David Delaney, President 3202 Dauphin St., Suite B Mobile, Alabama 36606 (205) 476-0700	Diversified	5
H&T Capital Corp. John R. Bloom, President 4750 Selma Highway P.O. Drawer Q Montgomery, Alabama 36105 (205) 288-6250	Diversified	5
ARIZONA		
American Business Capital Corp. Leonard A. Frankel, President 3550 North Central Ave. Suite 520 Phoenix, Arizona 85012 (602) 277-6259	Diversified	5
ARKANSAS		
First SBIC of Arkansas, Inc. Fred Burns, President Worthen Bank Building Suite 706 Little Rock, Arkansas 72201 (501) 378-1876	Diversified	1
Small Business Inv. Cap. Inc. Charles E. Toland, President 10003 New Benton Hwy. Mail to: P.O. Box 3627 Little Rock, Arkansas 72203 (501) 455-3590	Retail Grocers	4

LICENSEE	INVESTMENT POLICY	OWNER CODE
CALIFORNIA		
Asset Management Capital Co. Franklin Johnson, Jr., President 1411 Edgewood Dr. Palo Alto, California 94301 (415) 321-3131	Diversified	5
Brantman Capital Corp. William T. Brantman, President 2467 Mar East Mail to: P.O. Box 877 Tiburon, California 94920 (415) 435-4747	Diversified	5
Brentwood Assoc., Inc. Timothy Pennington 3rd, President 11661 San Vincente Blvd. Los Angeles, California 90049 (213) 826-6581	Diversified	3
Bryan Capital Corp. John M. Bryan, President 235 Montgomery St. Suite 2220 San Francisco, California 94104 (415) 421-9990	50% Major Group 36	5
Builders Capital Corp. Victor H. Indiek, President 2716 Ocean Park Boulevard Santa Monica, California 90404 (213) 450-0779	100% Major Group 15	5
California Northwest Fund, Inc. Kirk L. Knight, President 3000 Sand Hill Rd. Menlo Park, California 94025 (415) 854-2940	Diversified	2
California Partners Draper Assoc. CGP William H. Draper III, President Two Palo Alto Square, Suite 700 Palo Alto, California 94304 (415) 493-5600	Diversified	5-P
City Capital Corp. Morton Heller, President 9300 Wilshire Blvd., #328 Beverly Hills, California 90212 (213) 278-4080	Diversified	5
Continental Capital Corporation Frank G. Chambers, President 555 California St. San Francisco, California 94104 (415) 989-2020	100% Major Groups 35 & 36	6

LICENSEE	INVESTMENT POLICY	OWNER CODE
Crocker Capital Corp. Charles Crocker, President 111 Sutter St., Suite 600 San Francisco, California 94104 (415) 983-2156	66⅔% Major Group 36	2
Crocker Ventures Incorporated John M. Boyle, General Manager One Montgomery Street San Francisco, California 94104 (415) 983-7024	Diversified	1
Crosspoint Investment Corporaion Max S. Simpson, President 1015 Corporation Way Palo Alto, California 94303 (415) 964-3723	Diversified	3
Developers Equity Capital Corp. Larry Sade, Chairman of the Board 9201 Wilshire Blvd. Suite 204 Beverly Hills, California 90210 (213) 278-3611	100% Real Estate	5
Edvestco, Inc. William C. Edwards, President 150 Isabella Ave. Atherton, California 94025 (415) 421-9990	50% Major Group 36	5
Equilease Capital Corp. (Main Office; New York, N.Y.) 315 So. Beverly Drive Beverly Hills, California 90212		
First SBIC of California Tim Hay, President 333 South Hope St. Los Angeles, California 90017 (213) 613-5215	Diversified	1
Florists Capital Corporation Christopher M. Conroy, Chairman 10524 West Pico Blvd. Los Angeles, California 90017 (213) 836-6169	Diversified	5
Foothill Venture Corp. Russell B. Faucett, President 2049 Century Park East Los Angeles, California 90067 (213) 556-1222	Diversified	3

135

LICENSEE	INVESTMENT POLICY	OWNER CODE
Grocers Capital Co. Elliot Goldstone, Manager 2601 S. Eastern Ave. Los Angeles, California 90040 (213) 728-3322	Grocery Stores	4
H & R Investment Capital Co. Herman Christensen, President 801 American St. San Carlos, California 94070 (415) 365-4691	66⅔% Real Estate	5
Imperial Ventures Incorporated Richard D. Robins, V.P. & G.M. 9920 South Lacienega Blvd. Mail to: P.O. Box 92991, L.A. 90009 Inglewood, California 90301 (213) 649-3886	Diversified	1
Jermyn Venture Capital Corporation J. Barry Kulick, President 190 North Canon Drive Suite 400 Beverly Hills, California 90210 (213) 550-8819	Movie Specialist	5
Krasne Fund for Small Business, Inc. Clyde A. Krasne, President 9350 Wilshire Blvd., Suite 219 Beverly Hills, California 90212 (213) 274-7007	90% Real Estate	5
Marwit Capital Corp. Martin W. Witte, President 610 Newport Center Dr. Suite 480 Newport Beach, California 92660 (714) 640-6234	Diversified	5
Oceanic Capital Corp. Robert H. Chappell, President 350 California St., Suite 2090 San Francisco, California 94104 (415) 389-7677	Diversified	4
Professional SBIC David M. Zerner, President 9100 Wilshire Blvd. 8th Fl.–East Tower Beverly Hills, California 90212 (213) 274-5821	66⅔% Real Estate	5

LICENSEE	INVESTMENT POLICY	OWNER CODE
Roe Financial Corp. Martin J. Roe, President 9000 Sunset Blvd., Suite 412 Los Angeles, California 90069 (213) 275-4723	66⅔% Rental and Leasing	3
San Joaquin Capital Corporation Richard Robins, President 1675 Chester Ave., Third Floor Mail to: P.O. Box 1555 Bakersfield, California 93309 (805) 323-7581	Diversified	5
San Jose Capital Corp. H. Bruce Furchtenicht, President 100 Park Center Plaza San Jose, California 95113 (408) 293-7708	Diversified	5
Small Business Enterprises Co. Steven L. Merrill, President 555 California St. San Francisco, California 94104 (415) 622-2582	45% Major Groups 26 & 38	1
Union Venture Corp. Brent T. Rider, President 555 California St. San Francisco, California 94104 (415) 622-2582	Diversified	1
Walden Capital Corp. Arthur S. Berliner, President 303 Sacramento Street San Francisco, California 94109 (415) 391-7225	Diversified	2
Warde Capital Corp. (Main Office: Beverly Hills, CA) 3440 Wilshire Blvd. Los Angeles, California 90005		
Warde Capital Corp. Thomas R. Warde, President 8929 Wilshire Blvd., Suite 500 Beverly Hills, California 90211 (213) 657-0500	66⅔% Real Estate	4
Wells Fargo Investment Company Robert G. Perring, President 475 Sansome St. San Francisco, California 94111 (415) 396-3293	Diversified	1

LICENSEE	INVESTMENT POLICY	OWNER CODE
West Coast Venture Capital Gary W. Kalbach, President 10375 Bandley Drive Cupertino, California 95014 (408) 996-2702	Diversified	5-P
Westamco Investment Company Leonard G. Muskin, President 8929 Wilshire Blvd., Suite 400 Beverly Hills, California 90211 (213) 652-8288	66⅔% Real Estate	4
Western Bancorp Venture Cap. Co. Richard G. Shaffer, President 707 Wilshire Blvd. Suite 1850 Los Angeles, California 90017 (213) 614-5903	Diversified	1

COLORADO

Associated Capital Corporation Rodney J. Love, President 5151 Bannock Street Denver, Colorado 80216 (303) 534-1155	Grocery Stores	4
Central Investment Corp. of Denver (M.O.: Northwest Growth Fund, Inc. Minneapolis, Minn.) 811 Central Bank Bldg. Denver, Colorado 80202 (303) 825-3351		
Colorado SBIC Melvin J. Roberts, President 918 Seventeenth St. P.O. Box 5168 Denver, Colorado 80217 (303) 222-0465	Diversified	1
Davis Whittle Co. (The) Paul D. Whittle, President 885 Arapahoe Street Boulder, Colorado 80302 (303) 447-2642	Diversified	5
Denver Ventures, Inc. Fausto Miranda, President 4142 Tejon Street Denver, Colorado 80211 (303) 433-8636	Diversified	3

LICENSEE	INVESTMENT POLICY	OWNER CODE
Enervest, Inc. Mark Kimmel, President 5500 South Syracuse Circle Suite 269 Englewood, Colorado 80110 (303) 771-9650	Diversified	5
Euilease Capital Corp. (Main Office; New York, N.Y.) 120 Bryant Street Denver, Colorado 80219		

CONNECTICUT

LICENSEE	INVESTMENT POLICY	OWNER CODE
AB SBIC, Inc. Adam J. Bozzuto, President School House Road Cheshire, Connecticut 06410 (203) 272-0203	Retail Grocery Stores	4
All State Venture Capital Corp. Thomas H. Brown, Jr., President 830 Post Road East, P.O. Box 442 Westport, Connecticut 06880 (203) 226-9376	Diversified	6
Asset Capital and Management Corp. Ralph Smith, President 608 Ferry Blvd. Stratford, Connecticut 06497 (203) 375-0299	Diversified	5
Capital Assistance Corp. of Conn. Robert A. Foisie, President 33 Brook Street West Hartford, Connecticut 06110 (203) 232-6118	Diversified	5
Capital Resource Co. of Connecticut I. Martin Fierberg, President 345 North Main Street Suite 304 West Hartford, Connecticut 06117 (203) 232-1769	Diversified	5
Dewey Investment Corp. George E. Mrosek, President 101 Middle Turnpike West Manchester, Connecticut 06040 (203) 649-0654	Diversified	6

LICENSEE	INVESTMENT POLICY	OWNER CODE
First Connecticut SBIC David Engelson, President 177 State Street Bridgeport, Connecticut 06604 (203) 366-4726	50% Real Estate	6
First Miami SBIC (Main Office: Miami Beach, Fla.) 293 Post Road Orange, Connecticut 06477 (203) 227-6824		
J.H. Foster & Co. Ltd. FPI, Inc. John H. Foster, President 1010 Summer Street Stamford, Connecticut 06905 (203) 348-4385	Diversified	5-P
Manufacturers SBIC, Incorporated Frank D'Engenio, President 310 Main Street East Haven, Connecticut 06512 (203) 469-7901	Diversified	6
Marcon Capital Corp. Martin A. Cohen, President 49 Riverside Avenue Westport, Connecticut 06880 (203) 226-7751	Diversified	4
Nationwide Funding Corporation Neil H. Ellis, President 306 Progress Drive P.O. Box 209 Manchester, Connecticut 06040 (203) 646-6555	Diversified	5
Northern Business Capital Corp. Joseph W. Kavanewsky, President 7-9 Issac Street Norwalk, Connecticut 06850 (203) 866-1651	Diversified	5
Nutmeg Capital Corp. Leigh B. Raymond, V. President 35 Elm Street New Haven, Connecticut 06510 (203) 776-0643	Diversified	5
The SBIC of Connecticut, Inc. Kenneth F. Zarrilli, President 1115 Main Street Bridgeport, Connecticut 06603 (203) 367-3282	Diversified	6

LICENSEE	INVESTMENT POLICY	OWNER CODE
DISTRICT OF COLUMBIA		
Allied Investment Corporation George C. Williams, President 1625 Eye Street, N.W. Suite 603 Washington, D.C. 20006 (202) 331-1112	100% in Any One Industry	6
Capital Investment Co. of Washington Jay Goldberg, President 1010 Wisconsin Ave., N.W. Washington, D.C. 20007 (202) 333-5749	Diversified	5
Destan Capital Corporation Frank J. Defrancis, Chairman 4340 Connecticut Ave., N.W. Washington, D.C. 20008 (202) 362-1896	Diversified	5
Greater Washington Investors, Inc. Don A. Christensen, President 1015-18th St., N.W. Washington, D.C. 20036 (202) 466-2210	Diversified	6
Housing Capital Corp. George W. Defranceaux, Chairman 1133 Fifteenth St., N.W. Suite 700 Washington, D.C. 20005 (202) 857-5757	Operative Builders	4
FLORIDA		
Allied Capital Corp. (Main Office: Washington, D.C.) One Financial Plaza Suite 1614 Fort Lauderdale, Florida 33301		
Corporate Capital, Inc. Jerry Thomas, President 2001 Broadway Riviera Beach, Florida 33404 (305) 844-6070	Diversified	1

LICENSEE	INVESTMENT POLICY	OWNER CODE
First Miami SBIC Irve L. Libby, President 1195 N.E. 125 Street North Miami, Florida 33161 (305) 893-5537	50% Real Estate	5
First North Florida J.B. Higdon, President 107 North Madison St. P.O. Box 386 Quincy, Florida 32351 (904) 627-7188	Grocery Stores	5
Gold Coast Capital Corporation William I. Gold, President 3550 Biscayne Blvd., Room 601 Miami, Florida 33137 (305) 371-5456	Diversified	5
Lebaron Capital Corporation Roy Hess, President 4900 Bayou Blvd., Suite 106 Pensacola, Florida 32503 (904) 477-6207	Diversified	5
Market Capital Corp. E.E. Eads, President 1102 North 28th St. P.O. Box 22667 Tampa, Florida 33622 (813) 247-1357	Grocery Stores	4
Quiet SBIC (The) Alton Woody, President 105 East Garden Street Pensacola, Florida 32501 (904) 434-5090	Diversified	5
SBAC of Panama City, Florida J.R. Arnold, President 2612 West Fifteenth St. Panama City, Florida 32401 (904) 785-9577	80% in Lodging Places, Amusement, and Recreation	1
Southeast SBIC, Inc. Clement L. Hofmann, President 100 S. Biscayne Blvd. Miami, Florida 33131 (305) 577-3174	Diversified	1

142

LICENSEE	INVESTMENT POLICY	OWNER CODE
Suwannee Capital Corp. William Lovett, Chairman of Board 1010 East Adams St. Jacksonville, Florida 32202 (904) 355-8315	Retail Grocery Stores	5
GEORGIA Affiliated Investment Fund, Inc. Samuel Weissman, President 2225 Shurfine Drive College Park, Georgia 30337 (404) 766-0221	Retail Grocer	4
CSRA Capital Corp. (Main Office: Augusta, Ga.) 1401 West Paces Ferry Rd., N.W. Suite E116 Atlanta, Georgia 30327 (404) 231-1313		
CSRA Capital Corp. Allen F. Caldwell, Jr., President 1058 Claussen Road Augusta, Georgia 30907 (404) 736-2236	Diversified	2
Equilease Capital Corp. Main Office: New York, N.Y.) 22-61 Penimeter Pk., Suite 12 Atlanta, Georgia 30309		
Fidelity Capital Corp. Alfred F. Skiba, Vice Pres. & Treas. 380 Interstate North Suite 150 Atlanta, Georgia 30339 (404) 955-3880	100% Real Estate	3
First American Inv. Corporation Clifton Hofman, President 300 Interstate North Atlanta, Georgia 30339 (404) 955-0000	100% Real Estate	4
Investor's Equity, Incorporated I. Walter Fisher, President 2902 First National Bank Tower Atlanta, Georgia 30303 (404) 658-1002	Diversified	5
Mome Capital Corp. James A. Hutchinson, President 234 Main Street Thomson, Georgia 30824 (404) 595-1507	Mobile Homes	5

LICENSEE	INVESTMENT POLICY	OWNER CODE
Rio Investment Corp. John Mallory, General Manager 1415 Industry Avenue Albany, Georgia 31702 (912) 435-3575	Retail Grocery Stores	5
Southeastern Capital SBI Corp. J. Ray Efird, President Suite 505, Northcreek 3715 Northside Parkway, N.W. Atlanta, Georgia 30327 (404) 237-1567	Diversified	6

HAWAII

SBIC of Hawaii James Wong, Chairman of Board 1575 South Beretania St. Honolulu, Hawaii 96814 (808) 949-3677	66⅔% Real Estate	3

IDAHO

First Idaho Venture Cap. Corp. Dick Miller, Vice President Suite 1102, One Capital Center 999 Main Street, Drawer Y Boise, Idaho 83702 (208) 345-3460	Diversified	3

ILLINOIS

Abbott Capital Corp. Richard E. Lassar, President 120 South LaSalle St. Chicago, Illinois 60603 (312) 726-3803	Diversified	5
Adams Street Capital, Incorporated Marvin A. Marder, President 1866 Sheridan Rd., Suite 217 Highland Park, Illinois 60035 (312) 368-0077	Diversified	5
Advance Growth Capital Corporation Charles F. Sebastian, President Radio Center 9355 West Joliet Road La Grange, Illinois 60526 (312) 352-2650	Diversified	6
Agribusiness Capital Company James W. Erickson, President 1401 North Western Avenue Lake Forest, Illinois 60045 (312) 295-6300	Diversified	3

144

LICENSEE	INVESTMENT POLICY	OWNER CODE
Androck Capital Corp. John R. Anderson, President 1309 Samuelson Rd. Rockford, Illinois 61101 (815) 397-5000	Diversified	4
Certified Grocers Inv. Corporation Robert A. Korink, President 4800 South Central Avenue Chicago, Illinois 60638 (312) 585-7000	Retail Grocery Stores	4
Chicago Equity Corp. Morris Weiser, President One IBM Plaza, Suite 3625 Chicago, Illinois 60611 (312) 321-9662	Diversified	5
Continental Illinois Venture Corp. John L. Hines, President 231 South LaSalle St. Chicago, Illinois 60604 (312) 828-8023	Diversified	1
Equilease Capital Corp. (Main Office: New York, N.Y.) 2400 East Devon Des Plaines, Illinois 60018		
Evergreen Capital Corporation (Main Office: Houston, Texas) 208 South LaSalle Street Chicago, Illinois 60604		
First Capital Corp. of Chicago Stanley C. Golder, President One First National Plaza Chicago, Illinois 60670 (312) 732-8068	Diversified	1
Frontenac Capital Corp. Martin J. Koldyke, President 208 South LaSalle Street Chicago, Illinois 60604 (312) 368-0047	Diversified	2
Frontenac III Corp. David A.R. Dullum, President 208 South LaSalle Street Chicago, Illinois 60604 (312) 368-0044	Diversified	4

LICENSEE	INVESTMENT POLICY	OWNER CODE
Heizer Capital Corp. E.F. Heizer, President Suite 4100, 20 North Wacker Dr. Chicago, Illinois 60606 (312) 641-2200	Diversified	3
SB Management Investors, Inc. Kenneth Eaton, President 17 East Chestnut Chicago, Illinois 60611 (312) 943-0750	Diversified	5
United Cap. Corp. of Illinois Willard C. Mills, President United Center, State & Wyman Sts. P.O. Box 998 Rockford, Illinois 61105 (815) 987-2179	Diversified	4

INDIANA

	INVESTMENT POLICY	OWNER CODE
Tyler Refrigeration Capital Corp. William P. Linnen, President 2222 East Michigan Blvd. Michigan City, Indiana 46360 (616) 683-2000	Diversified	4

IOWA

	INVESTMENT POLICY	OWNER CODE
Moramerica Capital Corporation Robert Allsop, President Suite 200, American Bldg. Cedar Rapids, Iowa 52401 (219) 363-0263	Diversified	1

KANSAS

	INVESTMENT POLICY	OWNER CODE
Kansas Venture Capital, Inc. George L. Doak, President 1030 First National Bank Tower One Townsite Plaza Topeka, Kansas 66603 (913) 235-3437	Diversified	3

KENTUCKY

	INVESTMENT POLICY	OWNER CODE
Financial Opportunities, Inc. Anthony W. Foellger, President 981 South Third St. Louisville, Kentucky 40203 (502) 584-1281	Diversified	4

LICENSEE	INVESTMENT POLICY	OWNER CODE
Mountain Ventures, Incorporated Frederick J. Beste II, President 911 North Main Street Mail: P.O. Box 628, London, KY 40741 London, Kentucky 40741 (606) 864-5175	Diversified	5
LOUISIANA Caddo Capital Corporation Thomas L. Young, Jr., President 2924 Knight Street, Suite 335 Shreveport, Louisiana 71105 (318) 865-4629	Diversified	5
Capital for Terrebonne, Inc. Hartwell A. Lewis, President 1613 Barrow Street Houma, Louisiana 70360 (504) 868-3930	Diversified	5
Commercial Capital, Incorporated (Main Office: Covington, La.) 1809 West Thomas St. Hammond, Louisiana 70404 (504) 748-7157		
Commercial Capital, Incorporated Frederick W. Pierce, President P.O. Box 939 Covington, Louisiana 70433 (504) 892-4921	Diversified	3
Commercial Venture Cap. Corporation William H. Jackson, President 329 Texas Street Shreveport, Louisiana 71101 (318) 226-4602	Diversified	1
Dixie Business Investment Co. Steve K. Cheek, President 406 Lake St. Lake Providence, Louisiana 71254 (318) 559-1558	Diversified	2
First Business Investment Corp. Albert J. Prevot, President P.O. Box 1299 115 North Court Street Opelousas, Louisiana 70570 (318) 948-3115	Diversified	5

LICENSEE	INVESTMENT POLICY	OWNER CODE
First SBIC of Louisiana, Inc. Mrs. N. Hooper, Exec. V.P. 133 South Dorgenois St. New Orleans, Louisiana 70119 (504) 523-6705	Water Transportation	5
First Southern Capital Corporation Dennis Cross, President 6161 Perkins Rd., Suite 2C Mail to: P.O. Box 14205 Baton Rouge, Louisiana 70808 (504) 769-3004	Diversified	6
Louisiana Equity Capital Corp. G. Lee Griffin, President 451 Florida St. Baton Rouge, Louisiana 70801 (504) 389-4421	Diversified	1
Royal Street Inv. Corporation William D. Humphries, President Suite 4646, One Shell Square New Orleans, Louisiana 70139 (504) 588-9271	Diversified	4
Savings Venture Cap. Corporation Dale Anderson, President 6001 Financial Plaza P.O. Box 33888 Shreveport, Louisiana 71130 (318) 687-8996	Diversified	4
Venturtech Capital, Incorporated W.A. Bruce, Exec. V.P. Suite 706, Republic Tower 5700 Florida Blvd. Baton Rouge, Louisiana 70806 (504) 926-5482	Technology Field	4

MAINE

Great Northern Capital Corporation Barry Goldman, President 97A Exchange Place Portland, Maine 04111 (207) 773-1817	Diversified	5

MARYLAND

Real Estate Capital Corporation
(Main Office: Bala Cynwyd, Pa.)
9823 Central Avenue
Large, Maryland 20870
(301) 336-2345

LICENSEE	INVESTMENT POLICY	OWNER CODE
MASSACHUSETTS		
Advent Capital Corp. E. Roe Stamps, President 111 Devonshire St. Boston, Massachusetts 02109 (617) 725-2301	Diversified	5
Atlas Capital Corp. Herbert Carver, President 55 Court Street Boston, Massachusetts 02108 (617) 482-1218	50% Real Estate	3
Beacon Capital Corp. George S. Chaletzky, Treasurer 587 Beacon Street Boston, Massachusetts 02215 (617) 566-6000	50% Real Estate	5
Business Achievement Corporation Julian H. Katzeff, President 1280 Centre Newton Centre, Massachusetts 02159 (617) 965-0550	Diversified	5
Charles River Resources, Inc. Richard M. Burnes, Jr., President 133 Federal Street Boston, Massachusetts 02110 (617) 482-9370	Diversified	4
Devonshire Capital Corporation E. Roe Stamps, President 111 Devonshire Street Boston, Massachusetts 02109 (617) 725-2306	Diversified	5
Equilease Capital Corp. (Main Office: New York, N.Y.) 393 Totten Pond Rd., Suite 651 Waltham, Massachusetts 02154		
Federal Street Capital Corporation John H. Lamothe, President 75 Federal Street Boston, Massachusetts 02110 (617) 542-1380	Diversified	1
First Capital Corp. of Boston Richard A. Farrell, President 100 Federal Street Boston, Massachusetts 02110 (617) 434-2441	Diversified	1

LICENSEE	INVESTMENT POLICY	OWNER CODE
First United SBIC, Incorporated Alfred W. Ferrara, V. President 135 Will Drive Canton, Massachusetts 02021 (617) 828-6150	Diversified	4
Hellman, Gal Capital Corporation Frederick W. Hellman, Chairman One Federal Street Boston, Massachusetts 02110 (617) 482-7735	Diversified	3
International Film Investors (LP) (Main Office: New York, N.Y.) Suite 1400, One Federal Street Boston, Massachusetts 02110		
Massachusetts Capital Corporation David Harkins, President One Federal Street Boston, Massachusetts 02110 (617) 426-2488	Diversified	5
New England Enterprise Capital Corp. Z. David Patterson, Asst. V.P. 28 State St. Boston, Massachusetts 02106 (617) 742-0285	Diversified	1
Northeast Small Bus. Inv. Corp. Joseph Mindick, Treasurer 16 Cumberland St. Boston, Massachusetts 02115 (617) 267-3983	Diversified	5
Prime Capital Corp. Jason Rosenberg, President 10 Commercial Wharf South Suite 502 Boston, Massachusetts 02210 (617) 723-2103	Diversified	5
Schooner Capital Corp. Vincent Ryan, Jr., President 141 Milk Street Boston, Massachusetts 02109 (617) 357-9031	Diversified	5
Transatlantic Capital Corporation Bayard Henry, President 60 Batterymarch Street, Room 728 Boston, Massachusetts 02110 (617) 482-0015	Diversified	2

LICENSEE	INVESTMENT POLICY	OWNER CODE
UST Capital Corp. Stephen R. Lewinstein, President 40 Court St. Boston, Massachusetts 02108 (617) 726-7265	Diversified	1
Worcester Capital Corporation W. Kenneth Kidd, Manager 446 Main Street Worcester, Massachusetts 01608 (617) 853-7585	Diversified	1
Yankee Capital Corp. Richard F. Pollard, President 175 Federal Street Boston, Massachusetts 02110 (617) 482-1041	Diversified	1

MICHIGAN

Doan Resources Corp. Herbert D. Doan, President 110 East Grove Street Midland, Michigan 48640 (517) 631-2623	Diversified	3
Federated Capital Corporation Louis P. Ferris, Jr., President 20000 West Twelve Mile Road Southfield, Michigan 48076 (313) 557-9100	Diversified	3
Michigan Capital & Service, Inc. Joseph Conway, Manager 580 City Center Building Ann Arbor, Michigan 48104 (313) 663-0702	Diversified	2
Tyler Refrigeration Capital Corp. (Main Office: Michigan City, Ind.) 1329 Lake Street Niles, Michigan 49120		

MINNESOTA

Consumer Growth Capital, Inc. John T. Gerlach, President 430 Oak Grove, Suite 404 Minneapolis, Minnesota 55403 (612) 874-0694	Diversified	5

LICENSEE	INVESTMENT POLICY	OWNER CODE
Control Data Capital Corporation Edward E. Strickland, President 8100-34th Avenue South Bloomington, Minnesota 55420 (612) 853-8100	Diversified	4
Eagle Ventures, Inc. Lawrence L. Horsch, President Suite 700, Soo Line Building Minneapolis, Minnesota 55402 (612) 339-9694	Diversified	4
First Midwest Capital Corporation Alan K. Ruvelson, President 15 South Fifth St., Suite 700 Minneapolis, Minnesota 55402 (612) 339-9391	Diversified	3
North Star Ventures, Incorporated Gerald A. Rauenhorst, President Suite 1845 Northwestern Financial 7900 Xerxes Ave. South Minneapolis, Minnesota 55431 (612) 830-4550	Diversified	5
Northland Capital Corporation George G. Barnum, Jr., President 613 Missabe Building Duluth, Minnesota 55802 (218) 722-0545	Diversified	5
Northwest Growth Fund, Incorporated Daniel J. Haggerty, President 960 Northwestern Bank Building Minneapolis, Minnesota 55402 (612) 372-8770	Diversified	1
P.R. Peterson Venture Capital Corp. P.R. Peterson, President 3726 Oregon Avenue, South St. Louis Park, Minnesota 55426 (612) 935-3130	Diversified	5
Retailers Growth Fund, Incorporated E.O. Wack, President 5100 Gamble Dr. Minneapolis, Minnesota 55416 (612) 374-6250	Franchised Retailers	4
Westland Capital Corp. Robert S. Dunbar, President Suite 115 Hennepin Sq. 2021 East Hennepin Ave. Minneapolis, Minnesota 55413 (612) 331-9210	Diversified	6

	INVESTMENT POLICY	OWNER CODE

LICENSEE

MISSISSIPPI
De Soto Capital Corp.
William B. Rudner, President
8885 East Goodman
Olive Branch, Mississippi 38654
(601) 895-4145

| | Diversified | 5 |

Invesat Corporation
J. Thomas Noojin, President
162 E. Amite Street, Suite 204
Jackson, Mississippi 39201
(601) 969-3242

| | Diversified | 6 |

Vicksburg SBIC
Edward H. Russell, President
302 First National Bank Building
Vicksburg, Mississippi 39180
(601) 636-4762

| | Diversified | 5 |

MISSOURI
Atlas Small Business Investment Corp.
Ronald Jarvis, Jr., President
1617 Baltimore
Mail: P.O. Box 19657, K.C., Mo. 641
Kansas City, Missouri 64108
(816) 471-1750

| | Diversified | 4 |

Bankers Capital Corp.
Raymond E. Glasnapp, President
4049 Pennsylvania, Suite 304
Kansas City, Missouri 64111
(816) 531-1600

| | Diversified | 5 |

Capital for Business, Incorporated
James Linn, President
P.O. Box 13686
Kansas City, Missouri 64199
(816) 234-2344

| | Diversified | 1 |

Equilease Capital Corp.
7700 Clayton Road
St. Louis, Missouri 63117

Intercapco West, Inc.
Thomas E. Phelps, President
7800 Bonhomme Avenue
St. Louis, Missouri 63105
(314) 863-0600

| | Diversified | 4 |

LICENSEE	INVESTMENT POLICY	OWNER CODE

Moramerica Capital Corporation
(Main Office: Cedar Rapids, Iowa)
911 Main St., Suite 2710
Commerce Tower Bldg.
Kansas City, Missouri 64152

Moramerica Capital Corporation
(Main Office: Cedar Rapids, Iowa)
Suite 600, 111 West Port Plaza
St. Louis, Missouri 63141

NEVADA

Universal Investment Corporation	Diversified	5

Benard N. Nemerov, President
300 South Curry Street
Carson City, Nevada 89701
(702) 883-7585

NEW JERSEY

Capital SBIC, Inc.	85% Real Estate	5

Isadore Cohen, President
143 East State Street
Trenton, New Jerey 08608
(609) 394-5221

Delaware Valley SBIC
(Main Office: Phila., Pa.)
Plaza Apts.
Atlantic City, New Jersey 08201

Engle Investment Co.	Diversified	5

Murray Hendel, President
35 Essex St.
Hackensack, New Jersey 07601
(201) 489-3583

Eslo Capital	Diversified	5

Leo Katz, President
133 Washington St.
Morristown, New Jersey 07960
(201) 267-3152

Lloyd Capital Corp.	Diversified	6

Solomon Scharf, President
77 State Highway 5
P.O. Box 180
Edgewater, New Jersey 07020
(201) 947-6000

154

LICENSEE	INVESTMENT POLICY	OWNER CODE
Main Capital Inv. Corp. Sam Klotz, President 818 Main St. Hackensack, New Jersey 07601 (201) 489-2080	Diversified	5
Monmouth Capital Corp. Eugene W. Landy, President 125 Wyckoff Rd. 1st Merchants Bank Bldg., P.O. Box 335 Eatontown, New Jersey 07724 (201) 542-4927	Diversified	6
Quidnet Capital Corp. Stephen W. Fillo, President 909 State Rd. Princeton, New Jersey 08540 (609) 924-7665	Diversified	3
NEW MEXICO Albuquerque SBIC Albert T. Ussery, President 501 Tijeras Ave., N.W. P.O. Box 487 Albuquerque, New Mexico 87103 (505) 247-0145	Diversified	5
First Capital Corp. of New Mexico Shirley Ann Williams, President 8425 Osuna Rd., N.E. Albuquerque, New Mexico 87111 (505) 293-5057	Diversified	5
Fluid Capital Corp. George T. Slaughter, President 200 Lomas Blvd., N.W., Suite 527 Albuquerque, New Mexico 87110 (505) 255-7571	Diversified	4
Franklin Corp. (The) (Main office: New York, N.Y.) American Bank of Commerce Complex 200 Lomas Blvd., Suite 818 Albuquerque, New Mexico 87102		
New Mexico Capital Corp. William R. Christy, Exec. V.P. 2900 Louisiana Blvd., N.E. Suite 201 Albuquerque, New Mexico 87110 (505) 884-3600	Diversified	5

LICENSEE	INVESTMENT POLICY	OWNER CODE
Roger Cox SBIC Roger S. Cox, President 4121 Wyoming Blvd., N.E. Albuquerque, New Mexico 87111 (505) 293-3080	Diversified	5
Southwest Capital Inv., Inc. Roger L. Ford, President 8000 Pennsylvania Circle, N.E. Albuquerque, New Mexico 87110 (505) 265-9564	Diversified	3
Venture Capital Corp. of New Mexico Benirwin Bronstein, President 5301 Central Ave., N.E. Suite 1600 Albuquerque, New Mexico 87108 (505) 266-0066	Diversified	5

NEW YORK

LICENSEE	INVESTMENT POLICY	OWNER CODE
Amev Capital Corp. Allen R. Freedman, President 5 World Trade Center Suite 6281 New York, New York 10048 (212) 775-1912	Diversified	5
Atalanta Investment Co., Inc. L. Mark Newman, Chairman of Board 450 Park Ave. New York, New York 10022 (212) 834-1104	Diversified	4
Basic Capital Corp. Paul Kates, President 40 W. 37th St. New York, New York 10018 (212) 868-9645	Diversified	4
Beneficial Capital Corp. John Hoey, President 645 Fifth Ave. New York, New York 10022 (212) 752-1291	Diversified	5
Bohlen Capital Corp. Harvey J. Wertheim, President Suite 1260, 230 Park Ave. New York, New York 10017 (212) 867-9706	Diversified	5

156

LICENSEE	INVESTMENT POLICY	OWNER CODE
BT Capital Corp. William M. Eaton, President 600 Third Ave. New York, New York 10016 (212) 867-0606	Diversified	1
Canaveral Capital Corp. Michael Pratter, President 26 Court St., Suite 902 Brooklyn, N.Y. 11201 (212) 875-5216	Diversified	5
Capital for Future, Inc. (SBIC) Jay Schwamm, President 635 Madison Ave. New York, New York 10022 (212) 759-8060	50% Real Estate	3
Central New York SBIC (The) Robert E. Romig, President 351 So. Warren St. Syracuse, N.Y. 13202 (315) 469-7711	Vending Machine	4
Chase Manhattan Capital Corp. Robert Hubbard, President 1411 Broadway, 4th floor New York, New York 10018 (212) 223-7046	Diversified	1
Clarion Capital Corp. (Main office: Cleveland, Ohio) Two Penn Plaza New York, New York 10001		
CMNY Capital Co., Inc. Robert Davidoff, Vice President 77 Water St. New York, New York 10005 (212) 437-7078	Diversified	3
Edwards Capital Corp. Edward H. Teitlebaum, President 1 Park Ave., Room 1921 New York, New York 10016 (212) 686-2586	Diversified	5
Engle Investment Co. (Main office: Hackensack, N.J.) 135 W. 50th St. New York, New York 10020 (212) 757-9580		

LICENSEE	INVESTMENT POLICY	OWNER CODE
Equilease Capital Corp. Norbert Weissberg, President 750 Third Ave. New York, New York 10017 (212) 557-6880	Diversified	3
Equitable SBI Corp. David Goldberg, President 350 Fifth Ave., Suite 5820 New York, New York 10001 (212) 564-5420	66⅔% Health and Related	5
ESIC Capital, Inc. George Bookbinder, President 110 E. 59th St. Suite 1008 New York, New York 10022 (212) 421-1605	Diversified	5
European Development Capital Corp. Harvery J. Wertheim, President 230 Park Ave., Suite 1260 New York, New York 10017 (212) 867-9709	Diversified	5
Fairfield Equity Corp. Matthew A. Berdon, President 200 E. 42 St. New York, New York 10017 (212) 867-0150	Diversified	5
Fifty-third Street Ventures Alan J. Patricof, Chairman One E. 53rd St. New York, New York 10022 (212) 753-6300	Diversifed	5
First Connecticut SBIC (Main office: Bridgeport, Conn.) 68 Fifth Ave. New York, New York 10003		
First Wall St. SBIC, Inc. John W. Chappell, President 767 Fifth Ave., Suite 4403 New York, New York 10022 (212) 943-0987	Diversified	5

LICENSEE	INVESTMENT POLICY	OWNER CODE
FNCB Capital Corp. John Murphy, Asst. V.P. 399 Park Ave. New York, New York 10022 (212) 559-1127	Diversified	1
Franklin Corp. (The) Herman Goodman, President One Rockefeller Plaza Suite 2614 New York, New York 10022 (212) 581-4900	Diversified	6
Fundex Capital Corp. Howard Sommer, President 525 Northern Blvd. Great Neck, New York 11021 (516) 466-8551	Diversified	5
Hamilton Capital Fund, Inc. (The) Adolph Gross, President 555 Madison Ave. New York, New York 10022 (212) 838-8382	Diversified	5
Hanover Capital Corp. (The) Daniel J. Sullivan, President 223 E. 62nd St. New York, New York 10021 (212) 532-6670	Diversified	5
Intercoastal Capital Corp. Herbert Krasnow, President 380 Madison Ave. New York, New York 10017 (212) 986-0482	66⅔% Real Estate	6
Intergroup Venture Capital Corp. Ben Hauben, President 230 Park Ave. New York, New York 10017 (212) 661-5333	Diversified	5
International Film Investors, L.P. Josiah H. Child, Jr. President—Corporate General Partner 595 Madison Ave., 11th Floor New York, New York 10022 (212) 832-1920	100% Movie Specialist	4-P

LICENSEE	INVESTMENT POLICY	OWNER CODE
Irving Capital Corp. Andrew McWethy, V.P. & Gen. Mgr. One Wall Street New York, New York 10015 (212) 487-3474	Diversified	1
Lake Success Capital Corp. Herman Schneider, President 5000 Brush Hollow Rd. Westbury, New York 11590 (516) 997-4300	Diversified	5
M & T Capital Corp. Harold M. Small, President One M & T Plaza Buffalo, New York 14240 (716) 842-4200	Diversified	1
Marwit Capital (Main Office: Newport Beach, Cal.) 6 East 43rd St. New York, New York 10017 (212) 867-3906		
Mid Atlantic Fund, Inc. William Morris, President 9 West 57th St. New York, New York 10019 (212) 421-3940	Diversified	5
Midland Capital Corp. Donald Price, Vice President 110 William St. New York, New York 10038 (212) 577-0750	Diversified	6
Multi-Purpose Capital Corp. Eli B. Fine, President 31 South Broadway Yonkers, New York 10701 (914) 963-2733	Diversified	5
Nelson Capital Corp. Irwin Nelson, President 591 Stewart Ave. Garden City, L.I., New York 11530 (516) 222-2555	Diversified	5
New Horizons Capital Corp. Jay Inglis, President 90 Broad St. New York, New York 10004 (212) 422-2595	Diversified	4

LICENSEE	INVESTMENT POLICY	OWNER CODE
NIS Capital Corp. Howard Blank, President 34 S. Broadway White Plains, New York 10601 (914) 428-8600	Diversified	4
NYBDC Capital Corp. Marshall R. Lustig, President 41 State Street Albany, New York 12207 (518) 463-2268	Diversified	4
Percival Capital Corp. George A. Simpson, President 300 East 42nd St., 2nd Floor New York, New York 10017 (212) 689-1540	Diversified	5
Peter J. Schmitt SBIC, Inc. William Wannstedt, President 678 Bailey Ave. Buffalo, New York 14206 (716) 825-1111	Retail Grocers	4
Pines Venture Capital Corp. Robert H. Pines, President 5 World Trade Center New York, New York 10048 (212) 432-1818	Diversified	5
Pioneer Investors Corp. James G. Niven, President One Battery Park Plaza New York, New York 10004 (212) 344-4490	Diversified	5
Preferential Capital Corp. Bruce Bayroff, Sec.-Treasurer 16 Court St. Brooklyn, New York 11241 (212) 855-2728	Diversified	5
Printers Capital Corp. Herbert Brandon, President 1 World Trade Center Suite 3169 New York, New York 10048 (212) 432-0750	Printing & Duplicating Firms	5

LICENSEE	INVESTMENT POLICY	OWNER CODE
R&R Financial Corp. Imre Rosenthal, President 1451 Broadway New York, New York 10036 (212) 564-4500	Diversified	3
Rand SBIC, Inc. Donald Ross, President Rand Building Buffalo, New York 14203 (716) 853-0802	Diversified	6
Realty Growth Capital Corp. Lawrence Benenson, President 575 Lexington Ave. New York, New York 10022 (212) 755-9043	100% Real Estate Specialist	5
Royal Business Funds Corp. S.P. Bonan, President 60 East 42nd St. New York, New York 10017 (212) 986-8463	100% Real Estate	6
SB Electronics Investment Co. Stanley Meisels, President 60 Broad St. New York, New York 10004 (212) 952-7531	Diversified	5
Sherwood Business Capital Corp. Lewis R. Eisner, President 770 King St. Port Chester, New York 10573 (914) 937-6000	Diversified	5
Southern Tier Capital Corp. Harold Gold, Secretary-Treasurer 55 South St. Liberty, New York 12754 (914) 292-3030	Major Group 70 (Hotels & Rooming Houses)	5
Sprout Capital Corp. Lawrence R. Johnson, President 140 Broadway New York, New York 10005 (212) 943-0300	Diversified	3
Tappan Zee Capital Corp. Karl Kirchner, President 120 North Main St. New City, New York 10956 (914) 634-8890	66⅔% Real Estate	5

162

LICENSEE	INVESTMENT POLICY	OWNER CODE
Telesciences Capital Corp. George E. Carmody, President 135 East 54th St. New York, New York 10022 (212) 935-2550	Diversified	4
Van Rietschoten Capital Corp. Harvey J. Wertheim, President Suite 1260, 230 Park Ave. New York, New York 10017 (212) 867-9705	Diversified	5
Vega Capital Corp. Victor Harz, President 10 East 40th St. New York, New York 10016 (212) 685-8222	Diversified	6
Venture SBIC, Inc. Arnold Feldman, President 249-12 Jericho Turnpike Bellerose, New York 11426 (212) 343-8188	Diversified	5
Winfield Capital Corp. Stanley M. Pechman, President 237 Mamaroneck Ave. White Plains, New York 10605 (914) 949-2600	Diversified	5
Wood River Capital Corp. Edward B. Ory, President 645 Madison Ave. New York, New York 10022 (212) 355-3860	Diversified	5

NORTH CAROLINA

Delta Capital, Inc. Alex B. Wilkins, Jr., President 202 Latta Arcade 320 South Tryon St. Charlotte, North Carolina 28202 (704) 372-1410	50% Real Estate	3
Heritage Capital Corp. J. Randolph Gregory, President 2290 Jefferson First Union Plaza Charlotte, North Carolina 28282 (704) 334-2867	50% Real Estate	3

LICENSEE	INVESTMENT POLICY	OWNER CODE
Lowcountry Investment Corp. (Main Office: Charleston Heights., S.C.) Vernon Ave. Kinston, North Carolina 28659		
Northwestern Capital Corp. Clyde R. Brown, President 924 B St. Mail: P.O. Box 310 North Wilkesboro, North Carolina 286 (919) 667-2111	Diversified	6
NORTH DAKOTA First Dakota Capital Corp. James S. Lindsay, President 317 South University Dr. Fargo, North Dakota 58102 (701) 237-0450	Diversified	5
OHIO Banc One Capital Corp. James E. Kolls, Vice President 100 East Broad St. Columbus, Ohio 43215 (614) 461-5832	Diversified	1
Capital Funds Corp. Gary Pease, Chief Inv. Officer 127 Public Square Cleveland, Ohio 44114 (216) 861-4000	Communications	1
Clarion Capital Corp. Peter Van Oosterhout, President Union Commerce Bank Bldg. Suite 2011 Cleveland, Ohio 44115 (216) 687-1096	Diversified	6
Community Venture Corp. Si Sokol, President 88 East Broad St. Suite 1520 Columbus, Ohio 43215 (614) 228-2800	Diversified	1

164

LICENSEE	INVESTMENT POLICY	OWNER CODE
Dycap, Inc. A.G. Imhoff, President 88 East Broad Street Suite 1980 Columbus, Ohio 43215 (614) 228-6641	Diversified	5
Evergreen Capital Corp. (Main Office: Houston, Texas) Three Commerce Park Square 23200 Chagrin Blvd. Cleveland, Ohio 44122		
Fourth Street Capital Corp. Robert H. Leshner, President 508 Dixie Terminal Bldg. Cincinnati, Ohio 45202 (513) 579-0414	Diversified	5
Greater Miami Inv. Services, Inc. Robert Meyer, President 3131 South Dixie Drive, Suite 505 Dayton, Ohio 45439 (513) 294-6124	Diversified	2
Gries Investment Corp. Robert D. Gries, President 2310 Terminal Tower Bldg. Cleveland, Ohio 44113 (216) 861-1146	Diversified	5
Intercapco, Inc. Ronald E. Weinberg, President One Erieview Plaza, 10th Floor Cleveland, Ohio 44114 (216) 241-7170	Diversified	5
National City Capital Corp. Michael Sherwin, President 623 Euclid Ave. Cleveland, Ohio 44114 (216) 861-4900	Diversified	1
Tamco Investors (SBIC), Inc. Nathan H. Monus, President 375 Victoria Rd. Youngstown, Ohio 44515 (216) 792-3811	Retail Grocers	4

LICENSEE	INVESTMENT POLICY	OWNER CODE
Tomlinson Capital Corp. John A. Chernak, Vice President 13700 Broadway Cleveland, Ohio 44125 (216) 663-3363	Miniature Supermarket	4

OKLAHOMA

Activest Capital Corp. George J. Records, Chairman 6212 N. Western Oklahoma City, Oklahoma 73118 (405) 840-5597	100% Real Estate	4
Alliance Business Investment Co. Barry Davis, President 500 McFarlin Bldg. Tulsa, Oklahoma 74103 (918) 584-3581	Diversified	5
Bartlesville Inv. Corp. James L. Diamond, President P.O. Box 548 Bartlesville, Oklahoma 74003 (918) 333-3022	Diversified	5
First Oklahoma Inv. Capital Corp. Eldon Beller, President 120 North Robinson Oklahoma City, Oklahoma 73102 (405) 272-4779	Diversified	1
First Venture Corp. Jon R.K. Tinkle, President Venture Building, The Quarters Bartlesville, Oklahoma 74003 (918) 333-8820	Diversified	1
Henderson Funding Corp. C.A. Henderson, President 2629 N.W. 39th Expressway Oklahoma City, Oklahoma 73112 (405) 947-5746	Diversified	5
Investment Capital, Inc. James J. Wasson, President 101 West Broadway Mail to: P.O. Box 1071 Cushing, Oklahoma 74023 (918) 225-5850	Diversified	5

LICENSEE	INVESTMENT POLICY	OWNER CODE
Oklahoma Capital Corp. Bill Daniel, Sr., President Suite 550 2200 Classen Blvd. Oklahoma City, Oklahoma 73106 (405) 525-5544	Diversified	5
Southwest Venture Capital, Inc. Donald J. Rubottom, President 1920 First Place Tulsa, Oklahoma 74103 (918) 584-4201	Diversified	5
United Business Capital, Inc. Carl Sherman, Treasurer One East Main P.O. Box 322 Idabel, Oklahoma 74745 (405) 286-7652	Diversified	5

OREGON

Cascade Capital Corp. (Main Office: Northwest Growth Fund, Inc., Minneapolis, Minn.) 1300 S.W. 5th St., Suite 3018 Portland, Oregon 97201 (503) 223-6622		
First Farwest Capital Fund, Inc. C.M. Armstrong, President 400 SW Sixth Ave., 2nd Fl. P.O. Box 4162 Portland, Oregon 97208 (503) 224-7740	Diversified	3
Northern Pacific Capital Corp. John J. Tennant, Jr., President 16075 S.W. Upper Boones Ferry Rd. Mail to: P.O. Box 1530 Tigard, Oregon 97223 (503) 245-3147	Diversified	5

PENNSYLVANIA

American Venture Capital Co. Clair A. Snyder, President Axe Wood West, Suite 200 Shippack Pike & Butler Pike Ambler, Pennsylvania 19002 (215) 643-5956	Diversified	5

LICENSEE	INVESTMENT POLICY	OWNER CODE
Capital Corp. of America Martin M. Newman, President 1521 Walnut St. Philadelphia, Pennsylvania 19102 (215) 563-7423	Diversified	6
Central Capital Corp. W.D. McElhinny, Chairman of Board 1097 Commercial Ave. Lancaster, Pennsylvania 17604 (717) 569-9650	Diversified	1
Equilease Capital Corp. (Main Office: New York, N.Y.) One Parkway Center, Rm. 213 Pittsburgh, Pennsylvania 19102		
Fidelity America SBIC Howard I. Green, President 2 Penn Center Plaza, Suite 1700 Philadelphia, Pennsylvania 91902 (215) 568-3550	Diversified	6
Osher Capital Corp. Leonard Cantor, President Wyncote House Township Line Rd. & Washington Lane Wyncote, Pennsylvania 19095 (215) 624-4800	Diversified	5
Pennsylvania Growth Inv. Corp. William L. Mosenson, President Two Gateway Center, Suite 277 Pittsburgh, Pennsylvania 15222 (412) 281-1403	Diversified	3
Real Estate Capital Corp. William J. Levitt, Jr., President 111 Presidential Blvd. Bala Cynwyd, Pennsylvania 19004 (215) 569-4400	100% Real Estate Specialists	5
Sharon Small Business Investment Co. H. David Rosenblum, President 385 Shenango Ave. Sharon, Pennsylvania 16146 (412) 981-1500	Grocery Store	4
TDH Capital Corp. J. Mahlon Buck, Jr., President 2 Radnor Corporate Center Radnor, Pennsylvania 19087 (215) 293-9787	Diversified	5

LICENSEE	INVESTMENT POLICY	OWNER CODE
RHODE ISLAND		
Industrial Capital Corp.	Diversified	1
Albert A.T. Wickersham, President		
111 Westminster St.		
Providence, Rhode Island 02903		
(401) 278-6770		
Narragansett Capital Corp.	Diversified	6
Arthur Little, President		
40 Westminster St.		
Providence, Rhode Island 02903		
(401) 751-1000		
SOUTH CAROLINA		
Charleston Capital Corp.	Diversified	5
Henry Yaschik, President		
P.O. Box 696, 134 Meeting St.		
Charleston, South Carolina 29402		
(803) 723-6464		
Falcon Capital Corp.	Diversified	5
Mona G. Sokol, President		
100 Broad St.		
Charleston, South Carolina 29401		
(803) 723-8624		
Floco Investment Co. Inc. (The)	Food Retailers	5
William H. Johnson, Sr., President		
P.O. Box 216		
Scranton, South Carolina 29561		
(803) 389-2731		
Lowcountry Investment Corp.	Grocery Store	4
Joseph T. Newton, Jr., President		
4444 Daley St., P.O. Box 10447		
Charleston, South Carolina 29411		
(803) 554-9880		
TENNESSEE		
C&C Capital Corp.	Diversified	1
Donald L. Jones, President		
City and County Bank Building		
One Regency Square		
Knoxville, Tennessee 37909		
(615) 637-9220		
Financial Resources, Inc.	Diversified	5
Milton Picard, Chairman of Board		
2211 Sterick Bldg.		
Memphis, Tennessee 38103		
(901) 527-9411		

LICENSEE	INVESTMENT POLICY	OWNER CODE

TEXAS
Alliance Business Investment Co.
(Main Office: Tulsa, Oklahoma)
2660 South Tower
Houston, Texas 77002

Allied Bancshares Capital Corp. D. Kent Anderson, President P.O. Box 3326 Houston, Texas 77001 (713) 224-6611	Diversified	1
Brittany Capital Corp. Robert E. Clements, President 2424 LTV Tower Dallas, Texas 75201 (214) 742-5810	Diversified	2
Cameron Financial Corp. A. Baker Duncan, President 1410 Frost Bank Tower San Antonio, Texas 78205 (512) 223-9768	Diversified	5
Capital Marketing Corp. Nathaniel Gibbs, Chairman of Board P.O. Box 225293 Dallas, Texas 75222 (214) 638-1913	Retail Grocers	4
Central Texas SBI Corp. Walter G. Lacy, Jr., President P.O. Box 829 Waco, Texas 76703 (817) 753-6461	Diversified	1
CSC Capital Corp. Clifford J. Osborn, President Suite 700, 12900 Preston Road Dallas, Texas 75230 (214) 233-8242	Diversified	6

LICENSEE	INVESTMENT POLICY	OWNER CODE
Dallas Business Capital Corp. Edgar S. Meredith, Sr., V.P. Suite 333, Meadows Bldg. 5646 Milton St. Dallas, Texas 75206 (214) 691-0711	Diversified	6
Diman Financial Corp. Don Mann, President 13601 Preston Rd., Suite 717E Dallas, Texas 75240 (214) 233-7610	Diversified	4
Energy Assets, Inc. Laurence E. Simmons, Exec. V.P. 1800 South Tower Pennzoil Place Houston, Texas 77002 (713) 236-9999	Various Firms in Energy Ind.	4
Enterprise Capital Corp. Paul Z. Brochstein, President Suite 465 W. Executive Plaza 4635 Southwest Freeway Houston, Texas 77027 (713) 626-7171	Diversified	5
Evergreen Capital Corp. Jeffery Garvey, Exec. V.P. 7700 San Felipe, Suite 180 Houston, Texas 77063 (713) 783-5003	Diversified	3
First Bancorp Capital, Inc. George F. Baum, Jr., President 100 North Main St. P.O. Box 613 Corsicana, Texas 75110 (214) 874-4711	Diversified	1
First Capital Corp. John R. Payne, President 7100 Grapevine Hwy., Suite 105 Fort Worth, Texas 76118 (817) 284-0166	Diversified	5
First Dallas Capital Corp. Eric C. Neuman, President Suite 245, First National Bank Bldg. P.O. Box 83385 Dallas, Texas 75283 (214) 744-8050	Diversified	1

LICENSEE	INVESTMENT POLICY	OWNER CODE
First Texas Investment Co. Lynn D. Rowntree, President 2700 S. Post Oak, Suite 250 Transco Tower Houston, Texas 77056 (713) 629-5512	Diversified	5
Great American Capital Investors, Inc. Albert S. Dillard, President 1006 Holliday St. Wichita Falls, Texas 76301 (817) 322-4448	Diversified	1
Grocers SBI Corp. Milton E. Levit, President 3131 East Holcombe Blvd. Suite 101 Houston, Texas 77021 (713) 747-7913	Retail Grocers	4
Mercantile Dallas Corp. James B. Gardner, President 1704 Main St. Dallas, Texas 75201 (214) 741-4181	Diversified	1
Permian Basin Capital Corp. Douglas B. Henson, President P.O. Box 1599 Midland, Texas 79701 (915) 683-4231	Diversified	1
Red River Ventures, Inc. Thomas H. Schnitzius, President 535 Houston Natural Gas Bldg. Houston, Texas 77002 (713) 658-9806	Diversified	3
Republic Venture Group, Inc. William R. Cain, President P.O. Box 225961 Dallas, Texas 75265 (214) 653-5942	Diversified	1
Rice Country Capital, Inc. William H. Harrison, Jr., Pres. P.O. Box 215 Eagle Lake, Texas 77434 (713) 234-2506	Diversified	1

LICENSEE	INVESTMENT POLICY	OWNER CODE
Rice Investment Co. Alvin Diamond, Secretary 3200 Produce Row Houston, Texas 77023 (713) 652-2015	Retail Grocers	5
San Antonio Venture Group, Inc. William A. Fagan, President 2300 West Commerce St. San Antonio, Texas 78207 (512) 223-3633	Diversified	4
SBIC of Houston (The) William E. Ladin, President 1510 Neils Esperson Bldg. Houston, Texas 77002 (713) 223-5337	Diversified	5
South Texas SBIC Arthur E. Buckert, Treasurer 120 South Main St. P.O. Box 1698 Victoria, Texas 77901 (512) 573-5151	Diversified	1
Texas Capital Corp. W. Grogan Lord, President 2424 Houston Natural Gas Bldg. 1200 Travis Street Houston, Texas 77002 (713) 658-9961	Diversified	4
Trammell Crow Investment Co. Henry W. Billingsley, President 2001 Bryan Tower Suite 3200 Dallas, Texas 75201 (214) 747-0643	100% Real Estate	5
TSM Corp. Joe Justice, General Manager 4171 North Mesa, Suite A-203 Mail: Box 9938, El Paso, TX 79990 (915) 533-6375	Diversified	5
West Central Capital Corp. Howard W. Jacob, President Suite 206 440 Northlake Center Dallas, Texas 75238 (214) 348-3969	Diversified	5

LICENSEE	INVESTMENT POLICY	OWNER CODE
VERMONT		
Mansfield Capital Corp. Stephen H. Farrington, President Mountain Road Stowe, Vermont 05672 (802) 253-9400	Diversified	5
SBIC of Vermont, Inc. Robert B. Manning, President 121 West St. Rutland, Vermont 05701 (802) 775-3393	Diversified	1
Vermont Investment Capital, Inc. Harold Jacobs, President Route 14, Box 84 South Royalton, Vermont 05068 (802) 763-8835	Diversified	5
VIRGINIA		
Inverness Capital Corp. Harry S. Flemming, President 424 N. Washington St. Alexandria, Virginia 22314 (703) 549-5730	Diversified	5
Metropolitan Capital Corp. F.W. Scoville, President 2550 Huntington Ave. Alexandria, Virginia 22303 (703) 960-4698	Diversified	4
SBI Corp. of Norfolk D.H. Burlage, President 1216 Granby St., Suite 3 Norfolk, Virginia 23510 (804) 625-0534	Diversified	4
Tidewater Industrial Capital Corp. Armand Caplan, President Suite 1424 United Virginia Bank Bldg. Norfolk, Virginia 23510 (804) 622-1501	Diversified	4
Tidewater SBI Corp. Charles M. Etheridge, President 740 Duke Street Duke Grace Bldg., Suite 520 Norfolk, Virginia 23510 (804) 627-2315	Diversified	4

LICENSEE	INVESTMENT POLICY	OWNER CODE
Virginia Capital Corp. Robert H. Pratt, President 801 East Main St. Richmond, Virginia 23219 (804) 644-5496	Diversified	6
WASHINGTON Market Acceptance Corp. Archie E. Iverson, President 1718 Northwest 56th St., Suite B Seattle, Washington 98107 (206) 782-7600	Diversified	5
Northwest Business Inv. Corp. C. Paul Sandifur, President 929 West Sprague Ave. Spokane, Washington 99204 (509) 838-3111	Diversified	5
Northwest Capital Inv. Corp. Dale H. Ziegler, Gen. Manager 1940-116th Ave., N.E. P.O. Box 3500 Bellevue, Washington 98009 (206) 455-3049	Diversified	5
Trans-Am Bancorp., Inc. Harold T. Wosepka, President 3211 N.E. 78th Street Vancouver, Washington 98665 (206) 574-4749	100% Real Estate	5
Washington Capital Corp. G.A. Scherzinger, Mgr & Asst V.P. 1417 Fourth Ave. P.O. Box 1770 Seattle, Washington 98111 (206) 682-5400	50% Real Estate	3
WISCONSIN 77 Capital Corp. Sheldon B. Lubar, President 777 East Wisconsin Ave. Suite 3060 Milwaukee, Wisconsin 53202	Diversified	5

LICENSEE	INVESTMENT POLICY	OWNER CODE
Bankit Financial Corp. Roy D. Terracina, Exec. V.P. 733 North Vanburen St. Milwaukee, Wisconsin 53202 (414) 271-5050	Grocery Stores	4
Capital Investments, Inc. Robert L. Banner, Vice President 515 West Wells St. Milwaukee, Wisconsin 53203 (414) 273-6560	Diversified	6
Certo Capital Corp. Howard E. Hill, President 6150 McKee Road Madison, Wisconsin 53707 (608) 271-4500	Retail Grocers	4
Moramerica Capital Corp. (Main Office: Cedar Rapids, Iowa) 710 N. Plankinton Ave. Suite 333 Milwaukee, Wisconsin 53203 (414) 276-3839		
Super Market Investors Inc. John W. Andorfer, President 11300 West Burleigh St. Mail: P.O. Box 473 Milwaukee 53201 Wauwautosa, Wisconsin 53222 (414) 453-6211	Retail Grocers	4
Wisconsin Capital Corp. Lawrence J. Kujawski, Gen. Manager 312 East Wisconsin Ave, Suite 308 Milwaukee, Wisconsin 53202 (414) 289-9893	Diversified	5

WYOMING

Capital Corp. of Wyoming, Inc. Larry J. McDonald, Exec. V.P. P.O. Box 612 145 South Durbin St. Casper, Wyoming 82602 (307) 234-5351	Diversified	3

SBIC
TOTALS BY STATES

STATE	Size 1	Size 2	Size 3	Size 4	Size 5	TOTAL PRIVATE CAP	TOTAL OBLIGATION TO SBA
Alabama	0	4	0	0	4	2,410,000	3,600,000
Alaska	0	0	0	0	0	0	0
Arizona	0	1	0	0	1	500,000	0
Arkansas	0	2	0	0	2	1,292,228	2,250,000
California	1	21	11	4	37	74,471,510	64,607,645
Colorado	1	3	1	0	5	3,527,761	1,000,000
Connecticut	2	11	1	1	15	15,322,450	33,112,878
Delaware	0	0	0	0	0	0	0
D.C.	0	2	3	0	5	7,196,685	18,971,926
Florida	1	5	4	0	10	10,644,504	18,844,112
Georgia	1	3	4	0	8	12,923,094	30,902,311
Hawaii	0	1	0	0	1	317,100	450,000
Idaho	0	1	0	0	1	500,000	1,000,000
Illinois	3	3	6	2	14	43,464,356	9,604,166
Indiana	0	1	0	0	1	303,000	0
Iowa	0	0	1	0	1	3,700,000	12,770,390
Kansas	0	0	1	0	1	1,075,240	0
Kentucky	0	1	1	0	2	1,800,000	2,000,000
Louisiana	1	7	4	0	12	9,502,825	14,589,998
Maine	0	1	0	0	1	504,000	0
Maryland	0	0	0	0	0	0	0
Massachusetts	3	6	10	0	19	29,888,444	30,559,227
Michigan	1	1	1	0	3	4,429,759	7,725,000
Minnesota	1	4	4	1	10	14,443,975	23,897,148
Mississippi	0	2	1	0	3	3,692,180	2,297,468
Missouri	1	2	1	0	4	3,479,750	1,580,000
Montana	0	0	0	0	0	0	0
Nebraska	0	0	0	0	0	0	0
Nevada	0	1	0	0	1	400,000	0
New Hampshire	0	0	0	0	0	0	0
New Jersey	1	3	3	0	7	7,777,409	13,934,434
New Mexico	0	5	2	0	7	6,795,939	17,657,500
New York	6	32	13	7	58	163,845,113	118,565,129
North Carolina	0	0	3	0	3	3,863,265	8,812,717
North Dakota	0	1	0	0	1	365,000	600,000
Ohio	2	6	3	1	12	16,620,085	22,170,965
Oklahoma	0	7	3	0	10	7,716,934	17,112,009
Oregon	0	1	1	0	2	1,516,000	2,744,514
Pennsylvania	2	4	3	0	9	10,305,313	5,439,830
Puerto Rico	0	0	0	0	0	0	0
Rhode Island	0	0	1	1	2	16,697,921	29,159,862
South Carolina	1	2	1	0	4	3,200,651	6,900,153
South Dakota	0	0	0	0	0	0	0
Tennessee	0	2	0	0	2	1,405,320	1,266,500
Texas	3	14	12	1	30	49,690,316	77,488,909
Utah	0	0	0	0	0	0	0
Vermont	1	1	1	0	3	1,698,010	550,000
Virginia	0	4	2	0	6	6,402,966	16,551,394
Washington	1	3	1	0	5	6,338,324	17,928,900
West Virginia	0	0	0	0	0	0	0
Wisconsin	0	4	2	0	6	7,327,445	13,063,200
Wyoming	0	1	0	0	1	310,000	0
TOTAL	33	173	105	18	329	557,664,872	649,708,285

SBIC
TOTALS BY PRIVATE CAPITAL SIZE CLASS

TOTAL PRIVATE CAPITAL SIZE CLASS	TOTAL NUMBER OF SBICS	TOTAL PRIVATE CAP	TOTAL OBLIGATIONS TO SBA
Size 1–Below $300,000	33	7,270,133	8,123,560
Size 2–$300001 to $1.MM	173	95,493,250	128,884,952
Size 3–$1.MM to $5.MM	105	243,373,219	352,038,883
Size 4–Over $5.MM	18	211,528,270	160,660,890
TOTAL	329	557,664,872	649,708,285

SBIC
TOTALS BY TYPE OF OWNERSHIP

TYPE OF OWNERSHIP	TOTAL NUMBER OF SBICS	TOTAL PRIVATE CAP	TOTAL OBLIGATIONS TO SBA
Bank dominated	50	181,204,445	133,647,110
Bank associated	10	17,973,272	19,019,303
Fianancial organization	34	58,616,299	70,218,751
Non-financial org.	55	70,295,137	85,170,296
Individually owned	150	123,967,238	162,356,823
40 Act company	30	105,608,481	179,296,002
TOTAL	329	557,664,872	649,708,285

SBIC
PRIVATE CAPITAL BY TYPE OF OWNERSHIP
PRIVATE CAPITAL SIZE CLASS

Type of ownership	Size 1		Size 2		Size 3		Size4	
	Num	Dollars	Num	Dollars	Num	Dollars	Num	Dollars
Bank dominated	2	450000	18	11639928	23	65765466	7	103349051
Bank associated	0	0	5	2995859	4	9567831	1	5409582
Financial org.	3	610000	13	6172027	17	39834272	1	12000000
Non-financial org.	6	1457750	31	17586554	16	33315027	2	17935806
Individually owned	22	4752383	98	52606759	29	55108096	1	11500000
40 Act company	0	0	8	4492123	16	39782527	6	61333831

PART II — Minority Enterprise SBICs (MESBICs)

LICENSEE	INVESTMENT POLICY	OWNER CODE
ALASKA		
Alyeska Investment Company W.J. Darch, President 1835 South Bragaw St. Anchorage, Alaska 99512 (907) 279-9584	Diversified	4
ARIZONA		
Associated Southwest Investors, Inc. F. Brent Stewart, General Manager 114 West Adams, Suite 719 Phoenix, Arizona 85003 (602) 252-3973	Diversified	4
ARKANSAS		
Capital Management Services, Inc. Louise Lingo, President 4801 North Hills Blvd. N. Little Rock, Arkansas 72116 (501) 758-4553	Diversified	5
Kar-Mal Venture Capital, Inc. Thomas Karam, President University Tower Bldg. Suite 917 Little Rock, Arkansas 72204	Diversified	4
CALIFORNIA		
Associates Venture Capital Corp. Walter P. Strycker, President 632 Kearny St. San Francisco, California 94108 (415) 379-0351	Diversified	5
Beauhan Minority Inv. Corp. Gerald E. Webb, President 2 Commercial Blvd. Novato, California 94947 (415) 479-4310	Insurance Agencies	5
Business Equity & Dev. Corp. Richardo J. Olivarez, General Manager 1411 West Olympic Blvd. Suite 200 Los Angeles, California 90015 (213) 385-0351	Diversified	4

LICENSEE	INVESTMENT POLICY	OWNER CODE
Equitable Capital Corp. John C. Lee, President 419 Columbus Ave. San Francisco, California 94133 (415) 982-4028	Diversified	5
Hub Enterprises, Ltd. John B. Lacoste, President 5874 Doyle St. Emeryville, California 94608 (415) 653-5707	Diversified	5
MCA New Ventures, Inc. Robert A. Simmons, President 100 Universal City Plaza Universal City, California 91608 (213) 985-4321	Entertainment	4
Minority Enterprise Funding, Inc. Howard D. Balshan, President 4061 East Whittier Blvd. Los Angeles, California 90023 (213) 269-7335	Diversified	5
Opportunity Capital Corp. of Calif. Charles E. Stanley, President 100 California St., Suite 714 San Francisco, California 94111 (415) 421-5935	Diversified	2
Space Ventures, Inc. William J. Smollen, President 3901 MacArthur Blvd. Newport Beach, California 92660 (714) 851-0855	Diversified	4
Unity Capital Corp. Frank W. Owen, President 3620 30th St., Suite B San Diego, California 92104 (714) 295-6768	Diversified	5
Yosemite Capital Inv. Co. J. Horace Hampton, President 448 Fresno St. Fresno, California 93706 (209) 485-2431	Diversified	5

CONNECTICUT

Cominvest of Hartford, Inc. Robert W. Beggs, Jr., President 18 Asylum St. Hartford, Connecticut 06103 (203) 246-7259	Diversified	1

LICENSEE	INVESTMENT POLICY	OWNER CODE
Hartford Community Capital Corp. Ms. Jan-Gee W. McCollam, President 777 Main St., 7th floor Attn: Jan-Gee McCollam Hartford, Connecticut 06115 (203) 728-2840	Diversified	2
DISTRICT OF COLUMBIA Amistad Dot Venture Capital, Inc. Percy E. Sutton, President 1325 18th St., NW, Suite 211-21 kWashington, D.C. 20036 (202) 466-4323	Communications & Transportation	5
District of Columbia Inv. Co. Joseph D. Jackson, President 1420 New York Ave., NW Suite 400 Washington, D.C. 20005 (202) 452-1030	Diversified	4
Fulcrum Venture Capital Corp. Stephen L. Lilly, President 2021 K St., NW Suite 701 Washington, D.C. 20006 (202) 833-9580	Diversified	3
Minority Broadcast Investment Corp. Walter Threadgill, President 1220 19th St., NW Suite 501 Washington D.C. 20036 (202) 296-3340	Radio Stations	5
SCI Media Ventures, Inc. Herbert P. Wilkins, President 1625 I St., NW, Suite 304 Washington, D.C. 20006 (202) 293-9428	Communications Media	4
FLORIDA Allied Investment Developers, Inc. Robert V. Milberg, President 9999 N.E. 2nd Ave., Room 304 Miami Shores, Florida 33138 (305) 757-6796	Fast Food Franchises	5

LICENSEE	INVESTMENT POLICY	OWNER CODE
Biscayne Capital Corp. Raul P. Masvidal, President 340 Biscayne Blvd. Miami, Florida 33101 (305) 374-7667	Diversified	5
Burger King MESBIC, Inc. Don Christopherson, President P.O. Box 520783 Biscayne Annex Miami, Florida 33152 (305) 274-7011	Burger King Franchises	4
Cuban Investment Cap. Co. Anthony G. Marina, President 7425 N.W. 79th St. Miami, Florida 33166 (305) 885-8881	Diversified	5
Feyca Investment Co. Felipe de Diego, President 1830 N.W. 7th St. Miami, Florida 33127 (305) 643-1822	Diversified	5
First American Lending Corp. (The) Roy W. Talmo, Chairman 1200 N. Dixie Highway Lake Worth, Florida 33460 (305) 947-6678	Diversified	1
Jets Venture Capital Corp. Larry D. Barnette, President 2721 Park St. Jacksonville, Florida 32205 (904) 384-3471	Diversified	5
Miami Capital Corp. Robert M. Entin, President 1674 Meridian Ave., Suite 300 Mail to: P.O. Box 2037 Miami Beach, Florida 33139 (305) 672-2113	Diversified	5
Safeco Capital, Inc. Rene J. Leonard, President 8770 S.W. 8th St. Miami, Florida 33174 (305) 551-0809	Diversified	5

LICENSEE	INVESTMENT POLICY	OWNER CODE
Universal Financial Services, Inc. Mrs. Gertrude Zipkin, President 225 N.E. 35th St. Miami, Florida 33137 (305) 573-7496	Diversified	5
Venture Opportunities Corp. A. Fred March, President 1438 Brickell Ave. Miami, Florida 33131 (305) 358-0359	Diversified	5
Verde Capital Corp. Steven J. Green, Chairman of Board 255 Alhambra Circle, Suite 720 Coral Gables, Florida 33134 (305) 448-6300	Diversified	5

GEORGIA

LICENSEE	INVESTMENT POLICY	OWNER CODE
Cotton Belt Investment Corp. Lynwood A. Maddox, President 4542 Memorial Dr. Decatur, Georgia 30032 (404) 292-2626	Diversified	5
Enterprises Now, Inc. Joseph E. Lowery, President 898 Beckwith St., S.W. Atlanta, Georgia 30314 (404) 753-1163	Diversified	4
Southern Investment & Funding Corp., Inc. George Eng, President 300 W. Peachtree St., N.W. Atlanta, Georgia 30308 (404) 522-9151	Diversified	5

HAWAII

LICENSEE	INVESTMENT POLICY	OWNER CODE
Pacific Venture Capital, Ltd. Michael J. Coy, President 1505 Dillingham Blvd. Honolulu, Hawaii 96817 (808) 847-6502	Diversified	4

ILLINOIS

LICENSEE	INVESTMENT POLICY	OWNER CODE
Amoco Venture Capital Co. Lyle E. Schaffer, President 200 E. Randolph Dr. Chicago, Illinois 60601 (312) 856-6523	Diversified	4

LICENSEE	INVESTMENT POLICY	OWNER CODE
Cedco Capital Corp. Frank B. Brooks, President 180 North Michigan Ave. Chicago, Illinois 60601 (312) 984-5950	Diversified	4
Chicago Community Ventures, Inc. Phyllis George, President 19 South LaSalle St., Rm. 1114 Chicago, Illinois 60603 (312) 726-6084	Diversified	4
Combined Opportunities Inc. Wallace Buya, President 300 North State St. Chicago, Illinois 60610 (312) 266-3050	Diversified	4
Neighborhood Fund, Inc. (The) Ronald A. Grzywinski, President 1950 E. 71st St. Chicago, Illinois 60649 (312) 648-8074	Diversified	1
NIA Corporation Chris H. Howard, V. President 2400 South Michigan Ave. Chicago, Illinois 60616 (312) 842-5125	Insurance Companies	4
Northern Capital Corp. Joseph Ducharme, President 1017 Walnut St. Batavia, Illinois 60510 (312) 879-7317	Diversified	5
Tower Ventures, Inc. Stanley C. Piket, General Manager Sears Tower, BSC 9-29 Chicago, Illinois 60684 (312) 875-9628	Diversified	4
Urban Fund of Illinois Inc., The Peter H. Ross, President 300 N. State St. Chicago, Illinois 60610 (312) 266-3050	Diversified	1

LICENSEE	INVESTMENT POLICY	OWNER CODE

INDIANA

Minority Venture Co., Inc.
Frederick L. Howard, General Manager
Knute Rockne Memorial Bldg.
P.O. Box 382
South Bend, Indiana 46624
(219) 283-1115

Diversified — 4

KENTUCKY

Equal Opportunity Finance, Inc.
Franklin Justice, Jr., V.P. & Manager
224 East Broadway
Louisville, Kentucky 40202
(502) 583-0601

Diversified — 4

LOUISIANA

Business Capital Corp.
David R. Burrus, President
1732 Canal St.
New Orleans, Louisiana 70112
(504) 581-4002

Diversified — 5

Edict Investment Corp.
Rev. Robert P. Morin, President
2908 S. Carrollton Ave.
New Orleans, Louisiana 70118
(504) 861-9521

Diversified — 4

Louisiana Venture Capital Corp.
Ben D. Johnson, President
315 North St.
Natchitoches, Louisiana 71457
(318) 352-9138

Diversified — 4

SCDF Investment Corp.
Rev. Albert J. McKnight, President
1006 Surrey St.
Lafayette, Louisiana 70501
(318) 232-3767

Diversified — 4

MARYLAND

Albright Venture Cap., Inc.
William A. Albright, President
8005 Rappahannock Ave.
Jessup, Maryland 20794
(301) 490-4441

Diversified — 5

LICENSEE	INVESTMENT POLICY	OWNER CODE
Baltimore Community Inv. Co. James Crockett, President Suite 110, Metro Plaza Baltimore, Maryland 21215 (301) 669-2863	Diversified	5
Minority Investments, Inc. Frederick L. Sims, President 8121 Georgia Ave., Suite 800 Silver Spring, Maryland 20901 (301) 585-3444	Diversified	6
MASSACHUSETTS Massachusetts Venture Capital Corp. Charles T. Grigsby, President 141 Milk St., Room 1115 Boston, Massachusetts 02109 (617) 426-0208	Diversified	2
W.C.C.I. Capital Corp. Michael W. Tierney, President 791 Main St. Worcester, Massachusetts 01610 (617) 791-3259	Diversified	4
MICHIGAN Dearborn Capital Corp. Robert C. Chambers, President P.O. Box 1729 Dearborn, Michigan 48121 (313) 337-8577	Diversified	4
Independence Capital Formation, Inc. Walter McMurtry, Jr., President 3049 East Grand Blvd. Detroit, Michigan 48202 (313) 875-7669	Diversified	4
Innercity Cap. Access Center, Inc. Walter M. McMurtry, Jr., President 3049 East Grand Blvd. Detroit, Michigan 48202 (317) 875-4700	Diversified	5
Metro-Detroit Inv. Co. William J. Fowler, President 18481 West Ten Mile Rd., Suite 202 Southfield, Michigan 48075 (313) 557-3818	Food Stores	4

186

LICENSEE	INVESTMENT POLICY	OWNER CODE
Motor Enterprises, Inc. James Kobus, Manager 3044 West Grand Blvd. Detroit, Michigan 48202 (313) 556-4273	Diversified	4
Prime, Inc. James Thomas, President 1845 David Whitney Bldg. Detroit, Michigan 48226 (313) 964-3380	Diversified	4
MINNESOTA Control Data Community Ventures Fund Philip J. Bifulk, President 8100 34th Ave., South Bloomington, Minnesota 55420 (612) 853-8100	Diversified	4
Sagera Venture Corp., Inc. Gerald A. Stone, President 2850 Metro Dr. Bloomington, Minnesota 55426 (612) 854-2258	Diversified	4
MISSISSIPPI Invesat Capital Corp. J. Thomas Noojin, President 162 East Amite St., Suite 204 Jackson, Mississippi 39201 (601) 969-3242	Diversified	6
Sun-Delta Cap. Access Center, Inc. Charles Bannerman, President 819 Main St. Greenville, Mississippi 38701 (601) 335-5291	Diversified	5
NEBRASKA Community Equity Corp. of Nebraska William C. Moore, President 5620 Ames Ave., Rm. 103 Omaha, Nebraska 68104 (402) 455-1500	Diversified	4

LICENSEE	INVESTMENT POLICY	OWNER CODE
NEW JERSEY		
Broad Arrow Investment Corp. Charles N. Bellm, President 33 South St. P.O. Box 2231R Morristown, New Jersey 07960 (201) 540-8018	Diversified	5
Rutgers Minority Inv. Co. Louis T. German, President 92 New St. Newark, New Jersey 07102 (201) 648-5287	Diversified	4
NEW MEXICO		
Associated Southwest Investors, Inc. F. Brent Stewart, General Manager 2425 Alamo S.E. Albuquerque, New Mexico 87106 (505) 842-5955	Diversified	4
NEW YORK		
American Asian Capital Corp. Howard H. Lin, President 79 Wall St., Rm. 907 New York, New York 10005 (212) 422-6880	Diversified	5
Amistad Dot Venture Capital, Inc. (Main Office: Washington, D.C.) 211 East 43rd St. New York, New York 10017 (212) 490-3970		
Bancap Corp. William L. Whitely, President 420 Lexington Ave., Rm. 2455 New York, New York 10017 (212) 687-6470	Diversified	1
Brooklyn Capital Corp. Isaac Raitport, President 1476 39th St. Brooklyn, New York 11218 (212) 436-1803	Diversified	5

188

LICENSEE	INVESTMENT POLICY	OWNER CODE
CEDC MESBIC, Inc. John L. Kearse, President 106 Main St. Hempstead, New York 11550 (516) 292-9710	Diversified	4
Coalition SBIC Corp. Reginald F. Lewis, President 99 Wall St. New York, New York 10005 (212) 269-4544	Diversified	4
Cohen Capital Corp. Edward H. Cohen, President 8 East 36th St. New York, New York 10016 (212) 689-9030	Diversified	5
CVC Capital Corp. Joerg G. Klebe, President 666 Fifth Ave. New York, New York 10019 (212) 246-1980	Television Industry	5
Equico Capital Corp. Clarence C. Loftin III, Exec. V.P. 1270 Ave. of the Americas Suite 912 New York, New York 10020 (212) 489-7033	Diversified	4
Exim Capital Corp. Victor K. Chun, President 489 Fifth Ave. New York, New York 10017 (212) 490-0250	Diversified	5
Ibero American Investors Corp. Domingo Garcia, President 954 Clifford Ave. Rochester, New York 14261 (716) 544-0450	Diversified	5
Intergroup Funding Corp. Ben Hauben, President 230 Park Ave. New York, New York 10017 (212) 661-5428	Diversified	5
Japanese American Cap. Corp. Stephen C. Huang, President 120 Broadway New York, New York 10005 (212) 964-4077	Diversified	5

LICENSEE	INVESTMENT POLICY	OWNER CODE
King SBI Corp. Neil Ritz, President 902 Ellicott Square Bldg. Buffalo, New York 14202 (716) 856-4413	Diversified	4
Merit Funding, Inc. Roger L. Cohen, President 60 East 42nd St. New York, New York 10017 (212) 697-9660	Diversified	5
Minority Equity Cap. Co., Inc. Patrick O. Burns, General Manager 275 Madison Ave. New York, New York 10016 (212) 686-9710	Diversified	4
North Street Capital Corp. Lee A. Archer, Jr., President 250 North St. White Plains, New York 10625 (914) 631-3000	Diversified	4
ODA Capital Corp. Philip Klein, Executive Director 82 Lee Ave. Brooklyn, New York 11211 (212) 963-9260	Diversified	5
Pioneer Capital Corp. James G. Niven, President One Battery Park Plaza 28th Floor New York, New York 10004 (212) 483-9127	Diversified	5
Situation Ventures Corp. Sam Hollander, President 67 Taaffe Place Brooklyn, New York 11205 (212) 438-4909	Diversified	5
Square Deal Venture Capital Corp. Mordechai Z. Feldman, President Lincoln & Jefferson Aves. Village of New Square, New York 10977 (914) 354-7774	Diversified	5

LICENSEE	INVESTMENT POLICY	OWNER CODE
Taroco Capital Corp. David R.C. Chang, President 120 Broadway New York, New York 10005 (212) 964-6877	Chinese Americans	5

NORTH CAROLINA

Vanguard Investment Company, Inc. James F. Hansley, President Suite 309, Pepper Bldg. Fourth and Liberty St. Winston-Salem, North Carolina 27101 (919) 724-3676	Diversified	4

OHIO

Glenco Enterprises, Inc. Dr. Lewis F. Wright, V.P. 1464 E. 105 St., Suite 101 Cleveland, Ohio 44106 (216) 721-1200	Diversified	5

OKLAHOMA

American Indian Inv. Opportunity, Inc.
(Main Office: Chicago, Ill.)
205 East Main St.
Norman, Oklahoma 73069

PENNSYLVANIA

Alliance Enterprise Corp. Shallie M. Bey, Jr., President 1616 Walnut St., Suite 802 Philadelphia, Pennsylvania 19103 (215) 972-4230	Diversified	4
Greater Philadelphia Venture Cap. Corp. Inc. J. Walton St. Clair, Jr., President 920 Lewis Tower Bldg. 225 South Fifteenth St. Philadelphia, Pennsylvania 19102 (215) 732-3415	Diversified	2

PUERTO RICO

North America Inv. Corp. Carlos J. Pou, President Banco De Ponce Bldg. 19th Floor Hato Rey, Puerto Rico 00918 (809) 751-6161	Diversified	5

LICENSEE	INVESTMENT POLICY	OWNER CODE
TENNESSEE		
Chickasaw Capital Corp. Wayne J. Haskins, President 67 Madison Ave., Suite 813 P.O. Box 387 Memphis, Tennessee 38103 (901) 523-6404	Diversified	1
R.P.B. Investment Enterprises, Inc. M. Hall Oakley, President Falls Bldg. 22 North Front St. Memphis, Tennessee 38103 (901) 526-0063,	Diversified	5
Tennessee Equity Capital Corp. Richard Kantor, President 711 Union St. Nashville, Tennessee 37219 (615) 256-1331	Diversified	5
Tennessee Venture Capital Corp. David O. Kardokus, President 170 Fourth Ave. North Rm. 622 Nashville, Tennessee 37219 (615) 244-6935	Diversified	5
TEXAS		
MESBIC Financial Corp. of Houston Peter D. Sterling, President 717 Travis, Suite 600 Houston, Texas 77002 (713) 228-8321	Diversified	2
MESBIC Financial Corp. of Dallas Walter W. Durham, President 7701 N. Stemmons Freeway Suite 850 Dallas, Texas 75247 (214) 637-0445	Diversified	2
MESBIC of San Antonio Inc. A. John Yoggerst II, Vice President 2300 West Commerce San Antonio, Texas 78207 (512) 225-4241	Diversified	5

192

LICENSEE	INVESTMENT POLICY	OWNER CODE
VIRGINIA		
East West United Inv. Co.	Diversified	5
Bui Trac, Chairman		
6723 Whittier Ave., Suite 205B		
McLean, Virginia 22101		
(703) 821-6616		
Norfolk Investment Co., Inc.	Diversified	4
Kirk W. Saunders, General Manager		
Suite 515, Granby Mall Bldg.		
201 Granby St.		
Norfolk, Virginia 23510		
(804) 623-1042		
WASHINGTON		
Model Capital Corp.	Diversified	4
Jerome W. Page, President		
c/o Seattle Urban League		
105 14th Ave.		
Seattle, Washington 98122		
(206) 447-3799		
WEST VIRGINIA		
Lico MESBIC Investment Co.	Diversified	5
Edward T. Liu, President		
350 Ragland Rd.		
Beckley, West Virginia 25801		
(304) 252-5942		
WISCONSIN		
SC Opportunities, Inc.	Swiss Colony Franchises	5
Robert L. Ableman, Secretary		
1112 Seventh Ave.		
Monroe, Wisconsin 53566		
(608) 328-8400		

APPENDIX C

This section presents a sample license application form (first page only is shown) and the complete exhibits--required to be attached to such a form--as a guide for those who want to establish a Small Business Investment Company. The content of the exhibits, which follow the outline in the printed application form, is the most important part of the filing process; the wording shown here, though an accurate model that can be applied to a specific situation, should be carefully checked out with an attorney before filing. Hub City Investments, Inc. is a totally imaginary corporation.

LICENSE APPLICATION

(License Application under
The Small Business Investment Act of 1958, as amended.)

See Information and General Instructions, SBA Form 415B, as well as specific instructions on each item.

Date of Application ___June 16, 1980___

Item 1. *Name of License Applicant as Specified in Charter*

(Note: The corporate name should be such as not to misinform or mislead the public as to the purpose and function of the company. The name should not include the words "United States," "National," "Federal," "Reserve," "Bank," "Government," or "Development." The name should not be so similar to that of another organization as to imply association therewith without prior approval from such organization. The name must be approved by the Small Business Administration.)

HUB CITY INVESTMENTS, INC.

Item 2. *Location of License Applicant*

(Note: See § 107.101(b) of the Regulations. Give full address below, and by separate exhibit a brief description of size and type of space and information on rent. The office location can be in the same office building as that of another Licensee, but should otherwise be physically separated from any other Licensee. If the location is within the offices of another entity, there should be at least one room devoted solely to Licensee use. Licensee's name should appear on a street-level sign or building directory. No branch office or agency should be established without SBA approval.)

Street and No. ___297 Marlborough Street___

City and State ___Boston, Massachusetts___

County ___Middlesex___

Zip Code ___02116___ Telephone ___(617) 266-5189___

Item 3. *Capitalization*

(Note: See § 302(a) of the Small Business Investment Act. The minima therein prescribed are exclusive of organization expense. If there is more than one class of capital stock, supplement this schedule accordingly.)

( ) Proforma   ( ) Actual as of _____
                        Check One

Capital Stock

No. of shares authorized	300,000
Par value (x) or stated value ( ) per share	$ 10
No. of shares issued and fully paid	100,500
Issue price per share	$ 10
Paid-in capital and paid-in surplus	$ 1,005,000
Less organization expense, actual or estimated	$ 5,000
Net paid-in capital and paid-in surplus	$ 1,000,000

Give a brief summary description of each class of stock, outlining voting rights and any provisions relating to dividends, liquidation, preemption, conversion, redemption, assessments, or limitations on disposition.

HUB CITY INVESTMENTS, INC.

Item 2—Location of License Applicant

Arrangements have been made for approximately 450 square feet of office space. It is anticipated that rent will be approximately $900 per month, under a standard commercial lease. The office will be appropriately identified and will be an entity by itself (or explain its relationship to any other entity).

Item 3—Capitalization

The total number of shares of common stock which the corporation shall have authority to issue is three hundred thousand (300,000) and the par value of each of such shares is Ten Dollars ($10.00) amounting in the aggregate to Three Million Dollars ($3,000,000).

Each holder of capital stock of the corporation of whatever class shall have the first right to purchase shares and securities convertible into shares of capital stock of whatever class of the corporation that may hereafter be issued at any time (except for the first 100,500 shares) whether or not presently authorized, and including Treasury shares and shares issued for a consideration other than cash, in the ratio that the total number of shares of all classes of capital stock the holder owns at the time of the issue bears to the total number of shares of capital stock of all classes outstanding. This right shall be deemed waived by any holder of capital stock who does not exercise it by paying the full consideration for the stock preempted within ten days of receipt of a notice in writing from the corporation inviting him to exercise the right.

In all elections of directors of this corporation, each stockholder of record shall be entitled to as many votes as shall equal the number of votes which, except for this provision as to cumulative voting, he would be entitled to cast for the election of directors with respect to his shares multiplied by the number of directors to be elected, and he may cast all of such votes for a single director or may distribute them among the number to be voted for, or any two or more of them, as he may see fit.

Whenever a compromise or arrangement is proposed between this corporation and its creditors or any class of them and/or between this corporation and its stockholders or any class of them, any court or equitable jurisdiction within the State of Delaware may, on the application in a summary way of this corporation or of any creditor or stockholder thereof, or on the application of any receiver or receivers appointed for this corporation under the provisions of Section 291 of Title 8 of the Delaware Code or on the application of trustees in dissolution or of any receiver or receivers appointed for this corporation under the provisions of Section 279 of Title 8 of the Delaware Code order a meeting of the creditors or class of creditors, and/or of the stockholders or class of stockholders of this corporation, as the case may be, to be summoned in such a manner as the said court directs. If a majority in number representing three-fourths in value of the creditors or class of creditors, and/or of the stockholders or class of stockholders of this corporation, as the case may be, agree to any compromise or arrangement and to any reorganization of this corporation as consequence of such compromise or arrangement, the said compromise or arrangement and the said reorganization shall, if sanctioned by the court to which the said application has been made, be binding on all the creditors or class of creditors, and/or on all the stockholders or class of stockholders, of this corporation, as the case may be, and also on this corporation.

Notwithstanding any lesser requirement provided under any Delaware statute, the affirmative vote or consent of 66⅔ percent (or such greater percentage as may be required by statute) of all of the stockholders of the capital stock of the corporation, regardless of class, shall be required for the amendment of the following provisions of this Certificate:

(a) With respect to authorized shares and preemptive rights;

(b) With respect to cumulative voting; and

(c) With respect to greater voting requirements for amendments.

Notwithstanding any lesser requirement in the Delaware statutes, the corporation shall not approve any merger, consolidation or sale, lease or exchange of substantially all of its property or assets without the approval of fifty-five percent (or such greater percentage as may be required by the Delaware statutes) of the outstanding stock of the corporation entitled to vote thereon.

Item 4—Source of Initial Capital

(a) The $1,005,000 of private investment funds shown in Item 3 will be obtained through the sale of common stock to a maximum of 20 investors. Four of the said offerees will be officers and directors of the Applicant as shown in response to the question in Item 8(a). All of the said offerees will take said shares for investment purposes only. All offers will be made by personal contact. No salesmen, printed sales literature, newspaper or other advertising will be used.

(b) There will be no more than 20 beneficial owners of common stock at the completion of initial financing, reported in Item 3.

Item 5—Operating Area

The Applicant will conduct its operations principally in the Commonwealth of Massachusetts and in other areas within the United States of America and its territories and possessions as may from time to time be approved by the SBA as its operating territory, without regard, however, as to residence, domicile, place of business or location of the property of any small business or other parties with which it transacts its business or otherwise deals.

Item 6—Need for Licensee in Operating Area

There are numerous small business concerns in Boston and surrounding area in need of equity capital in the form of capital contribution or convertible loans. These businesses have found it difficult or impossible to obtain capital to finance operations and normal growth expansion. This is particularly true in the case of businesses which have been recently organized or which do not have a history of established earning capacity, or which cannot qualify for bank loans or collateralized loans. The applicant expects to be equity rather than collateral oriented in its investment decisions and, to a large extent, to invest in such businesses.

The Federal Reserve Bank of Boston in a recent issue of its Business Review says:

> Boston needs viable, active, aggressive SBICs to help fund small businesses with potential and add to the economic vitality of the area.

A copy of this issue is attached to this preliminary application as part thereof.

Item 7—Plan of Operations

In order to meet the diverse requirements of prospective applicants for financing and maintain sufficient flexibility, the Applicant will establish a broad financing policy.

The Applicant recognizes the need for both equities and loans. However, the Applicant will, as much as it is practicable, emphasize equity investments with particular attention to growth potentials. In other words, the Applicant will look to growth situations for the major portion of its return.

The Applicant intends to render management consulting services to clients and other small business concerns. Such services will be performed by Officers and Directors of the Applicant, and will include business consulting, appraising, feasibility reports, and placement of institutional loans.

The Applicant does not intend to use the services of an Investment Adviser (or describe the contemplated arrangement).

There is no affiliation or association between any officer, director, or general manager or 10% owner of the Applicant and any other licensee or the Investment Adviser of any other licensee (or describe fully such affiliations).

(In the case of a Sec. 301(d) MESBIC License Applicant, the following language should be included in Item 7:

The Applicant will make investments solely in small business concerns which will contribute to a well-balanced national economy by facilitating ownership in such concerns by persons whose participations in the free enterprise system is hampered because of social or economic disadvantages.

Note: If such Sec. 301(d) MESBIC Applicant is of minimum or near-minimum size from the standpoint of initial capital from private sources, a statement is required indicating that none of the private capital above a certain very small percentage (specifically designated) will be used to pay operating expenses of the licensee. The Applicant is to make clear that it is placing reliance on a commitment of the sponsoring company (or other identified organization committed to providing operation funding) to meet substantially all of the licensee's operating costs until the licensee can

198

assume such costs without, on that account, incurring a significant operating deficit.)

Item 8(a)—Management and Control

(All authorized shares represent common voting stock.)*

Name	Proposed Title or Relationship to Licensee	Rate of Compensation	Percent of Shares Beneficially Owned (All of Record) 5/29/80
John Cumber 297 Marlborough St. Boston, MA 02116	President (General Manager) and Director	$23,000 per annum	10%
Christian Maybern 10 Cedar Lane Way Boston, MA 02116	Vice President and Director	none	20%
Howell Burgess 44 Bow St. Cambridge, MA 02138	Secretary and Director	none	20%
Raymond Ditwell 76 Mt. Auburn St. Cambridge, MA 02138	Treasurer and Director	none	30%
James Kilbutton 51 Common St. Belmont, MA 02178	Director	none	none
Kendon Sulfitt 23 Pilgrim Pl. Boston, MA 02125	Director	none	none

Compensation will be paid to officers and directors of the Applicant in connection with services rendered by such officers and directors on behalf of the Applicant in the investigation of proposed investments, portfolio management, financial and administrative services, consulting and advising services to small business concerns and other SBIC's, and such other duties as may be assigned from time to time by the Board of Directors. In no event will the aggregate remuneration of all officers and directors, as a group, exceed $60,000 per annum, during the fiscal year ending March 31, 1981.

In addition, Mr. Cumber is to be granted an option exercisable at any time during a period of five years from the date of the grant to purchase up to an additional 1,000 shares of the Applicant's common stock at a price of $10 per share.

(The footnote immediately below relates to Item 8(a). Please note that it refers to preferred stock sold to private individuals or entities and has no reference to the preferred securities of qualifying Sec. 301(d) SBICs which may be purchased by SBA under Section 303(c) of the Small Business Investment Act of 1958 as amended by Public Law 92-595 approved October 27, 1972).

*A part of an Applicant's capital may consist of preferred stock, if desired. No part of any such preferred stock may be required to be redeemable by the Applicant, however, unless the following safeguards are included in the Applicant's Articles of Incorporation:

1. The private capital will not be reduced below the statutory minimum set forth in Section 302 of the Small Business Investment Act;
2. The ratio of Government funds to private capital will not exceed the statutory ratio set forth in Section 303 of the Act;
3. At the time of redemption, the company's capital will not be impaired, or rendered impaired by such redemption;
4. At the time of redemption, the company is not insolvent and such redemption will be permissible under state law, which permits redemptions only if the company would not be disabled by the redemptions to meet its obligations as they mature.

Item 8(b)—Management and Control

No shares of the applicant are indirectly owned or are to be indirectly owned by any other persons or entities than those set forth under Item 8(a).

No shares of the applicant are to be transferred or are to be resold to others under any existing or planned arrangements or agreements.

No shares of the applicant are now subject to or are to be made subject to any loan or pledge incident to the purchase thereof by those persons or entities set forth under Item 8(a).

No shares of the applicant are subject to or are to be subject to any understanding or commitment as to the exercise of voting rights under any existing or planned arrangements or agreements.

Item 9—Articles of Incorporation

(Note: The following text refers to the laws of Delaware, where many SBICs are incorporated; the language actually used should conform to the laws of the state of incorporation whether it is Delaware or another state--Ed.)

I, the undersigned, for the purpose of forming a corporation under and pursuant to the provisions of the laws of the State of Delaware for the purposes expressed in ARTICLE 3 hereof, do hereby adopt the following Articles of Incorporation.

ARTICLE I

The name of the corporation is HUB CITY INVESTMENTS, INC.

ARTICLE II

The address of incorporation is its registered office in the State of Delaware at No. 100 West Tenth Street, in the City of Wilmington, County of New Castle. The name of its registered agent at such address is The Corporation Trust Company.

ARTICLE III

This corporation is organized and chartered solely for the purpose of operating under the Small Business Investment Act of 1958, as amended, and will operate in the manner and shall have the powers, responsibilities and be subject to the limitations provided by said Act and the regulations issued by the Small Business Administration thereunder.

Subject to the foregoing, the powers and authority of the corporation shall be in general to possess and exercise all the powers and privileges granted by the General Corporation Law of Delaware or by any other law of Delaware or by this certificate of incorporation together with any powers incidental thereto.

Said specific powers and authority shall be as follows:

(a) To operate under the name set forth in ARTICLE I above;

(b) To issue in consideration for cash or such other consideration permitted by the Regulations the number of shares of stock indicated in ARTICLE IV;

(c) To borrow money and issue its debenture bonds, promissory notes, or other obligations under such general conditions and subject to such limitations and regulations as the Small Business Administration may prescribe;

(d) To provide equity capital to small business concerns (as defined by the Small Business Administration) under conditions authorized by section 304 of the Act and pertinent sections of the regulations, with the right to sell or dispose of securities so acquired in such a manner and under such terms and conditions as the Licensee shall determine;

(e) To make long-term loans (as defined by the Small Business Administration) to small business concerns (as defined by the Small Business Administration) for the purposes and in the manner and subject to the conditions described in section 305 of the Act; with the right to sell or dispose of such loans in such manner and under such terms and conditions as the Company shall determine;

(f) To acquire and make commitments for obligations and securities of a single enterprise only within the limitations established by section 306 of the Act, unless such limitations are waived by the Small Business Administration;

(g) To undertake its operations in cooperation with banks or other financial institutions, as contemplated under section 308(a) of the Act;

(h) To provide consulting and advisory services to small business concerns on a fee basis;

(i) To invest funds not reasonably needed for its current operations only in direct obligations of, or obligations guaranteed as to principal and interest by, the United States Government;

(j) To conduct its operations in accordance with and subject to regulations prescribed by the Small Business Administration;

(k) To submit to and pay for examinations made by direction of the Small Business Administration by examiners selected, employed, or approved by the Small Business Administration;

(l) To make reports to the Small Business Administration at such times and in such form as the Small Business Administration may require;

(m) To conduct its operations under the Act (specify area or areas); without limitation, however, as to the residence, domicile, or place of business of parties with which it transacts its business or otherwise deals in accordance with regulations issued by SBA;

(n) To regulate its business and conduct its affairs in a manner not inconsistent with the Act and regulations prescribed by the Small Business Administration thereunder;

(o) To adopt and use a corporate seal;

(p) To have succession for a period of not less than 30 years subject to dissolution in accordance with the laws of the State of Delaware and subject to forfeiture of its License from the Small Business Administration for violation of law or of regulation issued under the Act;

(q) To make contracts;

(r) To sue and be sued, complain, and defend in any court of law or equity;

(s) By its Board of Directors, to appoint such officers and employees as may be deemed proper, define their authority and duties, fix their compensation, require bonds of such of them as it deems advisable and fix the penalty thereof, dismiss such officers or employees, or any thereof, at pleasure, and appoint others to fill their places;

(t) To adopt bylaws regulating the manner in which its stock shall be transferred, its officers and employees appointed, its property transferred, and the privileges granted to it by law exercised and enjoyed;

(u) To maintain its principal office at 297 Marlborough Street, Boston, Massachusetts, 02116 and to establish branch offices or agencies within its operating ter-

ritory, subject to the approval of the Small Business
Administration;

(v) To acquire, hold, operate, and dispose of any property
(real, personal, or mixed) whenever necessary or appropriate to the carrying out of its lawful functions;

(w) To exercise such incidental powers as may reasonably be
necessary to carry out the business for which the corporation is established.

ARTICLE IV

(a) The total number of shares of common stock which the corporation
shall have authority to issue is three hundred thousand (300,000) and the
par value of each of such shares is Ten Dollars ($10.00) amounting in the
aggregate to Three Million Dollars ($3,000,000).

(b) Each holder of the capital stock of the corporation of whatever
class shall have the first right to purchase shares and securities convertible into shares of capital stock of whatever class of the corporation
that may hereafter be issued at any time (except for the first 100,500
shares) whether or not presently authorized, and including Treasury
shares and shares issued for a consideration other than cash, in the ratio
that the total number of shares of all classes of capital stock the holder
owns at the time of the issue bears to the total number of shares of capital
stock of all classes outstanding. This right shall be deemed waived by any
holder of capital stock who does not exercise it by paying the full consideration for the stock preempted within ten days of receipt of a notice in
writing from the corporation inviting him to exercise the right.

ARTICLE V

In all elections of directors of this corporation, each stockholder
of record shall be entitled to as many votes as shall equal the number of
votes which, except for this provision as to cumulative voting, he would be
entitled to cast for the election of directions with respect to his shares
multiplied by the number of directors to be elected, and he may cast all of
such votes for a single director or may distribute them among the number to
be voted for, or any two or more of them, as he may see fit.

ARTICLE VI

The name and mailing address of the incorporator is as follows:
  John Cumber
  297 Marlborough Street
  Boston, Massachusetts 02116

ARTICLE VII

The corporation is to have a perpetual existence.

ARTICLE VIII

Whenever a compromise or arrangement is proposed between this corporation and its creditors or any class of them and/or between this corpor-

ation and its stockholders or any class of them, any court of equitable jurisdiction within the State of Delaware may, on the application in a summary way of this corporation or of any creditor or stockholder thereof, or on the application of any receiver or receivers appointed for this corporation under the provisions of Section 291 of Title 8 of the Delaware Code or on the application of trustees in dissolution or of any receiver or receivers appointed for this corporation under the provisions of Section 279 of Title 8 of the Delaware Code order a meeting of the creditors or class of creditors, and/or of the stockholders or class of stockholders of this corporation, as the case may be, to be summoned in such a manner as the said court directs. If a majority in number representing three-fourths in value of the creditors or class of creditors, and/or of the stockholders or class of stockholders of this corporation, as the case may be, agree to any compromise or arrangement and to any reorganization of this corporation as consequence of such compromise or arrangement, the said compromise or arrangement and the said reorganization shall, if sanctioned by the court to which the said application has been made, be binding on all the creditors or class of creditors, and/or on all the stockholders or class of stockholders, of this corporation, as the case may be, and also on this corporation.

ARTICLE IX

Notwithstanding any lesser requirement provided under any Delaware statute, the affirmative vote or consent of 66⅔ percent (or such greater percentage as may be required by statute) of all the stockholders of the capital stock of the corporation, regardless of class, shall be required for the amendment of the following provisions of this Certificate:

(a) Article 4 with respect to authorized shares and pre-emptive rights;

(b) Article 5(a) with respect to cumulative voting; and

(c) This Article 9 with respect to greater voting requirements for amendments.

ARTICLE X

Notwithstanding any lesser requirement in the Delaware statutes, the corporation shall not approve any merger, consolidation or sale, lease or exchange of substantially all of its property or assets without the approval of fifty-five percent (or such greater percentage as may be required by the Delaware statutes) of the outstanding stock of the corporation entitled to vote thereon.

I, THE UNDERSIGNED, being the incorporator hereinbefore named, for the purposes of forming a corporation pursuant to the General Corporation Law of the State of Delaware, do make this certificate, hereby declaring and certifying that this is my act and deed and the facts herein stated are true, and accordingly have hereunto set my hand this 4th day of April, 1980.

John Cumber

STATE OF   )
                    ss.:
COUNTY OF   )

BE IT REMEMBERED that on this 4th day of April, 1980, personally came before me, a Notary Public for the County and State aforesaid, JOHN CUMBER, the party to the foregoing certificate of incorporation, known to me personally to be such, and acknowledged the said certificate to be the act and deed of the signer and that the facts stated therein are true.

GIVEN under my hand and seal of office the day and year aforesaid.

SEAL

Item 10—By-Laws

ARTICLE I

Stockholders

Section 1.1 Annual Meetings. An annual meeting of stockholders shall be held for the election of directors at such date, time and place, either within or without the State of Delaware, as may be designated by resolution of the Board of Directors from time to time. Any other business may be transacted at the annual meeting.

Section 1.2 Special Meetings. Special meetings of stockholders may be held at any time upon call of the Chairman of the Board, if any, the President or a majority of the Board of Directors, at such time and place either within or without the State of Delaware as may be stated in the call and notice. A special meeting of stockholders shall be called by the Secretary upon the written request of stockholders who together own of record 25% of the outstanding stock of any class entitled to vote at such meeting. Such request shall state the purpose of the meeting, which may be to elect a new Board of Directors.

Section 1.3 Notice of Meetings. Whenever stockholders are required or permitted to take any action at a meeting, a written notice of the meeting shall be given which shall state the place, date and hour of the meeting, and, in the case of a special meeting, the purpose or purposes for which the meeting is called. Unless otherwise provided by law, the written notice of any meeting shall be given not less than ten nor more than fifty days before the date of the meeting to each stockholder entitled to vote at such meeting. If mailed, such notice shall be deemed to be given when deposited in the United States mail, postage prepaid, directed to the stockholder at his address as it appears on the records of the corporation.

Section 1.4 Adjournments. Any meeting of stockholders, annual or special, may adjourn from time to time to reconvene at the same or at some other place and notice not be given of any such adjourned meeting if the time and place thereof are announced at the meeting at which the adjournment is taken. At the adjourned meeting the corporation may transact any business which might have been transacted at the original meeting. If the adjournment is for more than thirty days, or if after the adjournment a new record date is fixed for the adjourned meeting, a notice of the adjourned meeting shall be given to each stockholder of record entitled to vote at the meeting.

Section 1.5 Quorum. At each meeting of stockholders, except where otherwise provided by law or the certificate of incorporation or these by-laws, the holders of twenty-five percent of the outstanding shares of each class of stock entitled to vote at the meeting, present in person or by proxy, shall constitute a quorum. In the absence of a quorum, the stockholders so present may, by majority vote, adjourn the meeting from time to time in the manner provided by section 1.4 of these by-laws until a quorum shall attend.

Section 1.6 Organization. Meetings of stockholders shall be presided over by the Chairman of the Board, if any, or in his absence by the President or in their absence by a Vice President, or in the absence of the foregoing persons by a chairman chosen at the meeting. The Secretary shall act as secretary of the meeting, but in his absence the chairman of the meeting may appoint any person to act as secretary of the meeting.

Section 1.7 Voting; Proxies. Unless otherwise provided in the certificate of incorporation, each stockholder entitled to vote at any meeting of stockholders shall be entitled to one vote for each share of stock held by him which has voting power upon the matter in question, except that in all elections of directors of the corporation, each stockholder of record shall be entitled to as many votes as shall equal the number of votes which, except for this provision as to cumulative voting, he would be entitled to cast for the election of directors with respect to his shares multiplied by the number of directors to be elected, and he may cast all of such votes for a single director or may distribute them among the number to be elected, and he may cast all of such votes for a single director or may distribute them among the number to be voted for, or any two or more of them, as he may see fit. Each stockholder entitled to vote at a meeting of stockholders or to express consent or dissent to corporate action in writing without a meeting may authorize another person or persons to act for him by proxy but no such proxy shall be voted or acted upon after three years from its date, unless the proxy provides for a longer period. Voting at meetings of stockholders need not be by written ballot and need not be conducted by inspectors unless the holders of a majority of the outstanding shares of all classes of stock entitled to vote thereon present in person or by proxy at such meeting shall so determine. If a quorum is present, the affirmative vote of a majority of the votes cast at such meeting on any matter other than the election of directors shall be the act of the stockholders unless the vote of a greater or lesser number of shares of stock is required by law or by the Certificate of Incorporation.

ARTICLE II

Board of Directors

Section 2.1 Number; Qualifications. The Board of Directors shall consist of three or more members. The number of directors shall be such as may be fixed from time to time by resolution of the Board of Directors. Directors need not be stockholders.

Section 2.2 Election; Resignation; Vacancies. Until the first annual meeting of stockholders or until successors or additional directors are duly elected and qualified, the Board shall consist of the persons elected by the incorporator. At the first annual meeting of stockholders and at each annual meeting thereafter, or at a special meeting called for that purpose, the stockholders shall elect directors, each to hold office until the next succeeding annual meeting or until his successor is elected and qualified or until his earlier resignation or removal. Any director may resign at any time upon written notice to the corporation. Any vacancy occurring in the Board of Directors for any cause may be filled by a majority of the remaining members of the Board of Directors, although such majority is less than a quorum, or by the vote of the stockholders at a meeting called for that purpose, and each director so elected shall hold office until the next succeeding annual meeting of stockholders or until his successor is elected and qualified or until his earlier resignation.

Section 2.3 Regular Meetings. Regular meetings of the Board of Directors may be held at such places within or without the State of Delaware and at such times as the Board of Directors may from time to time determine, and if so determined notices thereof need not be given.

Section 2.4 Special Meetings. Special meetings of the Board of Directors may be held at any time or place within or without the State of Delaware whenever called by the Chairman of the Board, if any, or by the President, or by any two of the Board of Directors. Reasonable notice thereof shall be given by the person or persons calling the meeting.

Section 2.5 Telephonic Meetings Permitted. Members of the Board of Directors, or any committee designated by the Board, may participate in a meeting of such Board or committee by means of conference telephone or similar communications equipment by means of which all persons participating in the meeting can hear each other, and participation in a meeting pursuant to this by-law shall constitute presence in person at such meeting.

Section 2.6 Quorum. At all meetings of the Board of Directors, one-third of the entire Board shall constitute a quorum for the transaction of business. Except in cases where the certificate of incorporation or these by-laws otherwise provide, the vote of a majority of the directors present at a meeting at which a quorum is present shall be the act of the Board of Directors.

Section 2.7 Organization. Meetings of the Board of Directors shall be presided over by the Chairman of the Board, if any, or in his absence by the President, or in their absence by a chairman chosen at the meeting. The Secretary shall act as secretary of the meeting, but in his absence the chairman of the meeting may appoint any person to act as secretary of the meeting.

Section 2.8 Interested Directors; Quorum. No contract or transaction between the corporation and one or more of its officers, or between the corporation and any other corporation, partnership, association, or other organization in which one or more of its directors or officers are directors or officers, or have a financial interest, shall be void or voidable solely for this reason, or solely because the director or officer is present at or participates in the meeting of the Board or committee thereof which authorizes the contract or transaction, or solely because his or their votes are counted for such purpose, if: (1) the material facts as to his relationship or interest and as to the contract or transaction are disclosed or are known to the Board of Directors or the committee, and the Board or committee in good faith authorizes the contract or transaction by the affirmative votes of a majority of the disinterested directors, even though the disinterested directors be less than a quorum; or (2) the material facts as to his relationship or interest and as to the contract or transaction are disclosed or are known to the stockholders entitled to vote thereon, and the contract or transaction is specifically approved in good faith by vote of the stockholders; or (3) the contract or transaction is fair as to the corporation as of the time it is authorized, approved or ratified, by the Board of Directors, a committee thereof, or the stockholders. Common or interested directors may be counted in determining the presence of a quorum at a meeting of the Board of Directors or of a committee which authorizes the contract or transaction.

ARTICLE III

Committees

Section 3.1 Committees. The Board of Directors may, by resolution passed by a majority of the whole Board, designate one or more committees, each committee to consist of one or more directors of the corporation. The Board may designate one or more directors as alternate members of any committee, who may replace any absent or disqualified member at any meeting of the committee. In the absence or disqualification of a member of a committee, the member or members thereof present at any meeting and not disqualified from voting, whether or not he or they constitute a quorum, may unanimously appoint another of the Board of Directors to act at the meeting in place of any such absent or disqualified member. Any such committee, to the extent provided in the resolution of the Board of Directors, shall have and may exercise all the powers and authority of the Board of Directors in the management of the business and affairs of the corporation, and may authorize the seal of the corporation to be affixed to all papers which require it; but no such committee shall have the power or authority to amend the certificate of incorporation of the corporation, to adopt an agreement of merger or consolidation, to recommend to the stockholders the sale, lease or exchange of all or substantially all of the corporation's property and assets, to recommend to the stockholders a dissolution of the corporation or a revocation of a dissolution, or to amend these by-laws; and unless the

208

resolution expressly so provides, no such committee shall have the power or authority to declare a dividend or to authorize the issuance of stock.

ARTICLE IV

Officers

Section 4.1 Executive Officers; Election; Qualifications; Term of Office; Resignation; Vacancies. The Board of Directors shall choose a President, a Secretary and a Treasurer and it may, if it so determines, choose a Chairman of the Board from among its members. The Board of Directors may also choose one or more Vice Presidents, one more more Assistant Secretaries and one more more Assistant Treasurers. Each such officer shall hold office until the first meeting of the Board of Directors after the annual meeting of stockholders next succeeding his election, and until his successor is elected and qualifed or until his earlier resignation or removal. Any officer may resign at any time upon written notice to the corporation. Any number of offices may be held by the same person. Any vacancy occurring in any office of the corporation by death, resignation, removal or otherwise may be filled for the unexpired portion of the term by the Board of Directors at any regular or special meeting.

Section 4.2 Powers and Duties of Executive Officers. The officers of the corporation shall have such authority and perform such duties in the management of the corporation as may be prescribed, as generally pertain to their respective offices, subject to the control of the Board of Directors. The Board of Directors may require any officer, agent or employee to give security for the faithful performance of his duties.

ARTICLE V

Stock

Section 5.1 Certificates. Every holder of stock shall be entitled to have a certificate signed by or in the name of the corporation by the Chairman of the Board of Directors, if any, or the President or a Vice President, and by the Treasurer, or an Assistant Treasurer, or the Secretary or an Assistant Secretary, of the corporation, certifying the number of shares owned by him in the corporation. If such certificate is countersigned (1) by a transfer agent other than the corporation or its employee, or (2) by a registrar other than the corporation or its employee, any other signature on the certificate may be a facsimile. In case any officer, transfer or registrar who has signed or whose facsimile signature has been placed upon a certificate shall have ceased to be an officer, transfer agent or registrar before such certificate is issued, it may be issued by the corporation with the same effect as if he were such officer, transfer agent, or registrar at the date of issue.

Section 5.2 Lost, Stolen or Destroyed Stock Certificates; Issuance of New Certificates. The corporation may issue a new certificate of stock in the place of any certificate theretofore issued by it, alleged to have been lost, stolen or destroyed, and the corporation may require the owner of the lost, stolen or destroyed certificate, or his representative, to give the corporation a bond sufficient to indemnify it against any claim that may be made against it on account of the alleged loss, theft or destruction of any such certificate or the issuance of such new certificate.

ARTICLE VI

Miscellaneous

Section 6.1 Fiscal Year. The fiscal year of the corporation shall be determined by resolution of the Board of Directors.

Section 6.2 Seal. The corporate seal shall have the name of the corporation inscribed thereon and shall be in such form as may be approved from time to time by the Board of Directors.

Section 6.3 Indemnification of Directors, Officers and Employees. The corporation shall indemnify to the full extent authorized by law any person made or threatened to be made a party to an action or proceeding, whether criminal, civil, administrative or investigative, by reason of the fact that he, his testator or intestate is or was a director, officer, or employee of the corporation or serves or served any other enterprise as a director, officer or employee at the request of the corporation.

Section 6.4 Internal Control. The Board of Directors of the corporation shall adopt a plan of organization as required by the Regulations of the Small Business Administration, and shall supervise the implementation of such plan of organization, in order to safeguard the assets of the corporation and to check the accuracy and reliability of its financial data. Such plan of organization shall cover the corporation's personnel, portfolio of investment securities, funds and equipment. Such plan of organization shall also provide for dual control over disbursement of funds and withdrawal of securities from safekeeping as required by such Regulations.

Section 6.5 Fidelity Insurance. A fidelity bond shall be maintained in the form and amount, covering such officers and employees, as required by the Regulations of the Small Business Administration.

Section 6.6 Form of Records. Any records maintained by the corporation in the regular course of its business, including the stock ledger, books of account, and minute books, may be kept on, or be in the form of, punch cards, magnetic tape, photographs, microphotographs, or any other information storage device, provided that the records so kept can be converted into clearly legible form within a reasonable time. The corporation shall so convert any records so kept upon the request of any person entitled to inspect the same.

Section 6.7 Amendment of By-Laws. These by-laws may be altered or repealed, and new by-laws made, by two-thirds of the members of the Board of Directors or by the holders of two-thirds of the stock of the corporation entitled to vote thereon.

THE UNDERSIGNED, as Secretary of HUB CITY INVESTMENTS, INC., does hereby certify that the foregoing is a true copy of the By-laws of the corporation.

WITNESS my hand and seal of HUB CITY INVESTMENTS this 16th day of June, 1980.

SEAL

_____

Howell Burgess, Secretary

Item 11—Certified Copy of Organization Action
of Incorporator by which present Directors Elected.

THE UNDERSIGNED, as Secretary of HUB CITY INVESTMENTS, INC., does hereby certify that annexed hereto is a true copy of the organization action of the sole incorporator of the Corporation dated May 10, 1980, and does further certify that the directors elected thereby constitute the entire Board of Directors and none of said directors has been removed, replaced or has resigned as of the date hereof.

WITNESS my hand and seal of HUB CITY INVESTMENTS, INC. CORPORATION this 16th day of June, 1980.

_____

Howell Burgess, Secretary

ORGANIZATION ACTION BY INCORPORATOR WITHOUT A MEETING

The following action permitted to be taken at the organization meeting of the incorporator of HUB CITY INVESTMENTS, INC. is hereby taken without a meeting:

(a) A certified copy of the certificate of incorporation, filed by the Secretary of State of Delaware on April 11, 1980, and lodged for recordation in the office of the Recorder of Deeds of the County of New Castle immediately thereafter on the same day as required by law, is hereby directed to be inserted in the minute book preceding this instrument.

(b) By-Laws relating to the business of the corporation, the conduct of its affairs, its rights or powers and the rights and powers of its shareholders, directors and officers, in the form attached, are hereby adopted as and for the by-laws of the corporation, and a copy thereof, appended to this instrument, is hereby directed to be inserted in the minute book.

(c) The following persons are hereby elected directors of the corporation to hold office until the first annual meeting of shareholders:

John Cumber
Christian Maybern

                    Howell Burgess
                    Raymond Ditwell
                    James Kilbutton
                    Kendon Sulfitt

        (d) This instrument, signed by the incorporator, is hereby
directed to be inserted in the minute book immediately following the copy of the certificate of incorporation.

Dated: May 10, 1980

                                        _____
                                        John Cumber, Incorporator

        *Item 12—Certified Copy of Unanimous Consent of Directors
        in Lieu of a Meeting by which Current Officers Elected.*

        THE UNDERSIGNED, as Secretary of HUB CITY INVESTMENTS, INC., does
hereby certify that annexed hereto is a true copy of the unanimous consent
of the directors of the Corporation in lieu of a first meeting dated as of
May 11, 1980 and does further certify that the officers elected thereby are
each and every officer of the Corporation and none of said officers has been
removed, replaced or has resigned as of the date hereof.
        WITNESS my hand and seal of HUB CITY INVESTMENTS, INC., this 16th day
of June, 1980.

                                        _____
                                        Howell Burgess, Secretary

            CONSENT OF DIRECTORS IN LIEU OF FIRST MEETING

        The undersigned, being all the directors of HUB CITY INVESTMENTS,
INC., a corporation organized and existing under the laws of the State of
Delaware, do hereby give their written consent, pursuant to Section 141 of
the Delaware General Corporation Law, to the following:

        (1) the approval of the minutes of action taken by the sole in-
corporator of the Corporation on May 10, 1980;

        (2) the adoption of the following resolutions:

            RESOLVED, that the form of stock certificate at-
        tached hereto is hereby adopted as the form of stock
        certificate for this Corporation's capital stock, par
        value $10 per share; and it is further

            RESOLVED, that the seal, an impression whereof,
        is hereto attached, be adopted as the corporate seal of
        the Corporation.

212

(3) the election of the following persons to the offices set forth opposite their names to serve until such time as their successors shall have been elected and shall have qualified:

John Cumber	President
Christian Maybern	Vice President
Raymond Ditwell	Treasurer
Howell Burgess	Secretary

(4) The adoption of the following resolutions:

RESOLVED, that the Shawmut Bank of Boston be and hereby is designated as the depository of the funds of the Corporation and that the Bank's forms of resolutions attached hereto, providing, among other things, for the signature of two or more officers on all checks, be and they hereby adopted; and it is further

RESOLVED, that the Custodian Agreement between the Corporation and the Shawmut Bank, whereby the Shawmut Bank shall be custodian for the securities of the Corporation, be and hereby is approved in the form thereof attached hereto.

(5) The adoption of the following resolution:

RESOLVED, that the officers of the Corporation be and each of them hereby is authorized and directed for and on behalf of the Corporation to prepare a License Application to be executed and submitted to the Small Business Administration; and to take such further action and do such further things as such officer or officers deem necessary or desirable to obtain a license for the Corporation as a Small Business Investment Corporation under the aforementioned Act.

(6) The adoption of the following resolution:

RESOLVED, that the officers of the Corporation be and each of them hereby is authorized and directed, for and on behalf of the Corporation, to prepare, execute and file with the Secretary of the Commonwealth of Massachusetts an Application for Authority; and to take such further action and to do such further things as such officer or officers deem necessary or desirable to qualify the Corporation to do business in the Commonwealth of Massachusetts as a foreign corporation.

IN WITNESS WHEREOF, the undersigned have executed this consent as of the 11th day of May 1980.

Item 13—Certified Copy of Resolution of the Board of Directors
Authorizing Execution and Submission of this License Application

THE UNDERSIGNED, as Secretary of HUB CITY INVESTMENTS, INC., does hereby certify that by unanimous written consent of the Board of Directors of the Corporation dated as of May 11, 1980, the following resolution was adopted, and that said resolution has not been amended, annulled or revoked:

"RESOLVED, that the officers of the Corporation be and each of them hereby is authorized and directed for and on behalf of the Corporation to prepare a License Application under the Small Business Investment Act of 1958, as amended; to cause said application to be executed and submitted to the Small Business Administration; and to take such further action and do such further things as such officer or officers deems necessary or desirable to obtain a license for the Corporation as a Small Business Investment Corporation under the aforementioned Act."

WITNESS my hand and seal of HUB CITY INVESTMENTS, INC. this 16th day of June, 1980.

Howell Burgess, Secretary

Item 14—Name of Bank in which Cash is Deposited
and Name of Custodian of Securities

Concurrently with the issuance of the License, all of the Applicant's cash will be in a deposit account at Shawmut Bank of Boston, 1 Federal Street, Boston, Massachusetts 02116. (See Item 15). Shawmut Bank is also the custodian of the Applicant's securities. The Applicant has no other deposit account or custodian of securities.

Item 15—Letter from Depository Bank and Custodian Evidencing Cash and Securities on Deposit to the account of the Applicant.

Concurrently with the issuance of the License herein applied for, Applicant will deliver to the SBA the original of the form of letter attached hereto from Shawmut Bank of Boston.

(Letterhead of Shawmut Bank of Boston)

June   , 1980

Small Business Administration
1441 L Street, N.W.
Washington, D.C. 20416

Gentlemen:

Please be advised that this Bank holds in Deposit Account No.
for Hub City Investments, Inc., cash in the amount of $1,000,000 as of the date hereof.

There are no encumbrances or restrictions against such deposits.

The Bank is also the custodian of securities for Hub City Investments, Inc., but as of the date hereof is holding no securities for Hub City Investments, Inc.

Very truly yours,
SHAWMUT BANK OF BOSTON

By_____

Item 16—Letter to Securities and Exchange Commission

(Letterhead of Law Firm)

May 6, 1980

Securities and Exchange Commission
500 North Capitol Street
Washington, D.C. 20549

Re: Hub City Investments, Inc.

Gentlemen:

We are the attorneys for Hub City Investments, Inc. (the "Company"), a Delaware corporation organized solely for the purpose of operating as a Small Business Investment Company under the Small Business Investment Act

215

of 1958, as amended (the "SBIA"). The Company intends to file a License Application with the Small Business Administration (the "SBA") as required by the SBIA in the near future. A draft of the proposed Application in substantially final form is attached hereto as Exhibit A. The general instructions of the SBA require that a letter from the Securities and Exchange Commission (the "SEC") be filed with the Application evidencing that the securities of the Applicant sold or proposed to be sold, as set forth in its License Application, are not required to be registered under the Securities Act of 1933 (the "1933 Act") and that the Applicant is not required to register as an investment company under the Investment Company Act of 1940 (the "1940 Act"); or if such registration is required, evidence satisfactory to the SBA that the Applicant has complied with such requirements. The general instructions of the SBA also direct that the Applicant or its counsel furnish certain information to the SEC. Pursuant to these instructions, the following facts are set forth:

1. The Company has one class of stock designated as Capital Stock, $10 par value. There are 300,000 shares of Capital Stock authorized, but as of the date hereof none of these shares has been issued. It is intended that 100,500 shares of said stock will be issued to investors at $10.00 per share for a total capitalization of $1,005,000. These investors have entered into, or will shortly enter into, an agreement, whereby they agree to subscribe to such shares pursuant to the terms and conditions therein set forth. The agreement also provides that each purchaser is acquiring such shares for his own account and not with a view to, or in connection with, any distribution of such stock, nor with any present intention of distributing such stock.

2. We have been advised that the total number of offerees of the stock of the Company, including the persons who will be actual investors, is less than twenty, all of whom were solicited by personal contact by John Cumber, an officer of Hub City Investments, Inc., one of the investors. No compensation was paid to any person for such solicitation. Also, no printed sales literature, newspaper or other advertising was used. All of the investors are either institutional investors or are individuals sophisticated in financial affairs.

3. No investor shall own 30% or more of the stock of the Company.

4. It is not presently intended that the Company will raise additional capital by the offer of any capital stock of the Company; however, it is contemplated that additional funds may be raised by the sale of debentures to the SBA or to institutional investors subject to the guarantee of the SBA to the extent permitted by the SBIA.

Based on the foregoing facts, it is our opinion (i) that the securities of the Company proposed to be sold, as set forth in its License Application, are not required to be registered under the 1933 Act by virtue of the exemption provided in Section 4(2) thereof, and (ii) that the Company is not required to register as an investment company under the 1940 Act by virtue of Section 3(c)(1) therof. Accordingly, we respectfully request on behalf of the Company and at its request, that the SEC issue to the Company a letter concurring in the foregoing conclusions as required by the SBA.

Respectfully submitted,

Item 17—Opinion of Counsel for the Applicant

(Letterhead of Law Firm)

June 16, 1980

Small Business Administration
1441 L Street, N.W.
Washington, D.C. 20416

Gentlemen:

We are the attorneys for Hub City Investments, Inc., a corporation organized and existing under the laws of the State of Delaware (the "Applicant"), in connection with its License Application under the Small Business Investment Act of 1958, as amended.

In this connection, we have examined the Certificate of Incorporation and the By-Laws of the Applicant to authorize execution and submission of the License Application, and such other documents as we deem relevant and necessary as a basis for the opinions hereafter set forth.

Based on the foregoing, it is our opinion that:

1. The Applicant has complied with all applicable local, State and Federal laws in the formation and organization of the Applicant.

2. The Applicant, in selling its stock to obtain the required capital and surplus, has complied with every law, regulation and obligation relating to or controlling the sale of its stock, and when the funds are paid to it by each entity in consideration for said stock (which stock is to be issued by the Applicant simultaneously with the issuance of the License by the Small Business Administration), Applicant shall be authorized and entitled to receive and retain such funds.

3. The Applicant is chartered by the appropriate authorities to conduct, in its proposed operating territory, or area, only the activities described under Title III of the Small Business Investment Act of 1958, as amended.

4. The Applicant is authorized and entitled to conduct said franchise powers in full in each jurisdiction to be named in its License as part, or all, of its operating territory, or area, immediately upon the issuance of a License.

Very truly yours,

Item 18—Names of Persons Assisting in Preparation of the Application

Legal services in connection with the preparation and presentation of this application have been and are being provided by Messrs. Fanshaw, Beebe, Labour and Vane, of Winter Street, Boston, Massachusetts 02108. It is estimated that the total compensation to be paid to said firm, including disbursements, in connection with the organization of the Applicant and the preparation of this application will be $5,000.

Item 19—Declaration of Applicant

We represent that the Licensee will be operated in full conformity with the Small Business Investment Act of 1958, as amended, and the Small Business Administration regulations pertaining thereto.

We have not and will not, directly or indirectly, use any funds advanced by any small business investment company to any small business concern, or use any funds available as a result of funds advanced by a small business investment company to a small business concern, to purchase any stock of the Licensee or for the purpose of repaying any obligation incurred in connection with the furnishing of funds to be used for the purchase of any stock of the Licensee.

We represent that the Licensee will not engage in any transaction with any of the persons or entities set forth in #107.1004 of the regulations except as permitted by the terms of said section.

We hereby certify that all information submitted in this Form 415 and in the exhibits submitted therewith, or in connection therewith, is true and correct to the best of the knowledge and belief of each one of us and that it is being submitted for the purpose of obtaining a license to operate as a small business investment company. We further agree that all statements made in this Form 415 and in the said exhibits are to be considered material for the purpose of inducing SBA to issue a license and to disburse SBA funds in reliance on the said statements.

HUB CITY INVESTMENTS, INC.

Corporate
Seal   By_____
                                              John Cumber
                                              President

_____dated this 16th day of June, 1980.
Secretary of Licensee

_____   _____
              John Cumber   Christian Maybern

_____   _____
            Howell Burgess   Raymond Ditwell

_____   _____
           James Kilbutton   Kendon Sulfitt

APPENDIX D

SBA REGIONAL OFFICE – INVESTMENT STAFF

Region I   Connecticut, Massachusetts, Maine, New Jersey, New Hampshire, Rhode Island, Vermont, District of Columbia

    Chief   William W. Leopold   (202) 653-6930

Region II   New York, Puerto Rico, Virgin Islands

    Chief   Lawrence F. Friess   (202) 653-6427

Regions III, IV   Alabama, Delaware, Florida, Georgia, Kentucky, Maryland, Mississippi, North Carolina, Pennsylvania, South Carolina, Tennessee, Virginia, West Virginia

    Chief   Anthony DiMuzio   (202) 653-6473

Regions V, VIII   Colorado, Illinois, Indiana, Michigan, Minnesota, Montana, North Dakota, Ohio, South Dakota, Utah, Wisconsin, Wyoming, Washington

    Chief   Jerome Dillon   (202) 653-6690

Regions VI, VII   Arkansas, Iowa, Kansas, Louisiana, Missouri, Nebraska, New Mexico, Oklahoma, Texas

    Chief   Richard Pippel   (202) 653-6926

Regions IX, X   Alaska, Arizona, California, Guam, Hawaii, Idaho, Nevada, Oregon

    Chief   Marvin D. Klapp   (202) 653-6935

APPENDIX E

ECONOMIC DEVELOPMENT ADMINISTRATION REGIONAL OFFICES

John E. Corrigan
Regional Director
Atlantic Regional Office
Federal Reserve Bank Building
105 No. 7th St., Rm. 600
Philadelphia, PA 19106

(215) 597-4603
Connecticut, Delaware, District
of Columbia, Maine, Maryland,
Massachusetts, New Hampshire, New
Jersey, New York, Pennsylvania,
Puerto Rico, Rhode Island,
Vermont, Virginia, Virgin
Islands, West Virginia

Charles E. Oxley
Regional Director
Southeastern Regional Office
Suite 700
1365 Peachtree St., NE
Atlanta, GA 30309

(404) 881-7401
Alabama, Florida, Georgia,
Kentucky, Mississippi, North
Carolina, South Carolina,
Tennessee

Craig M. Smith
Regional Director
Rocky Mountain Regional Office
Suite 505, Title Bldg.
900 17th St.
Denver, CO 80222

(303) 837-4714
Colorado, Iowa, Kansas, Missouri,
Montana, Nebraska, North Dakota,
South Dakota, Utah, Wyoming

(312) 353-7706
Illinois, Indiana, Minnesota,
Ohio, Michigan, Wisconsin

Ed Jeep
Regional Director
Midwestern Regional Office
175 W. Jackson Blvd.
Suite A-1630
Chicago, IL 60604

(206) 442-0596
Alaska, American Samoa, Arizona,
California, Guam, Hawaii, Idaho,
Nevada, Oregon, Washington,
Navajos (Arizona, Colorado, New
Mexico)

Phyllis Lamphere
Regional Director
Western Regional Office
Suite 500, Lake Union Bldg.
1700 Westlake Ave., No.
Seattle, WA 98109

(512) 397-5461
Arkansas, Louisiana, New Mexico,
Oklahoma, Texas

Joseph B. Swanner
Regional Director
Southwestern Regional Office
Suite 600, American Bank Tower
221 W. 6th St.
Austin, TX 78701

APPENDIX F
FARMERS HOME ADMINISTRATION

STATE OFFICES

ALABAMA
Elizabeth Wright
Rm. 717, Aronov Bldg.
474 So. Court St.
Montgomery, AL 36102
(205) 832-7077
FTX 534-7077

ALASKA
John R. Roderick
P.O. Box 1289
Palmer, AK 99645
(907) 745-2176

ARIZONA
Manuel O. Dominquez
Rm. 3433, Federal Bldg.
230 No. First Ave.
Phoenix, AZ 85025
(602) 261-6701
(Use same 7-digit no. for FTS)

ARKANSAS
Sherman Williams
5529 Federal Office Bldg.
700 W. Capitol
For letter mail:
P.O. Box 2778
Little Rock, AR 72203
(501) 378-6281
FTS 740-6281

CALIFORNIA
Lowell Pannell
459 Cleveland St.
Woodland, CA 95695
(916) 666-2650
FTS 448-3223

COLORADO
Ernest C. Phillips
Rm. 231, No. 1 Diamond Plaza
2490 W. 26th Ave.
Denver, CO 80211
(303) 837-4347
FTS 327-4347

DELAWARE
(Delaware, District of Columbia,
 Maryland)
John D. Daniello
151 E. Chestnut Hill Rd., Suite 2
Newark, DE 19713
(302) 573-6694
FTS 487-6694

FLORIDA
Michael R. Hightower
Federal Bldg.
401 SE 1st Ave., Rm. 214
For letter mail:
P.O. Box 1088
Gainesville, FL 32602
(904) 376-3218
FTS 946-7221

GEORGIA
Robert L. Blalock
355 E. Hancock Ave.
Athens, GA 30601
(404) 546-2162
FTS 250-2162

HAWAII
Megumi Kon
345 Kekuanaoa St.
Hilo, HI 96720
(808) 961-4781

IDAHO
Joe T. McCarter
Rm. 429, Federal Bldg.
304 No. 8th St.
Boise, ID 83702
(208) 384-1730
FTS 554-1318

ILLINOIS
John W. Linfield
2106 W. Springfield Ave.
Champaign, IL 61820
(217) 356-1891
FTS 958-9149

INDIANA
James E. Posey
Suite 1700
5610 Crawfordsville Rd.
Indianapolis, IN 46224
(317) 269-6415
FTS 331-6415

IOWA
Max L. McCord
Rm. 873, Federal Bldg.
210 Walnut St.
Des Moines, IA 50309

KANSAS
John T. Denyer
444 S.E. Quincy St.
Topeka, KS 66683
(913) 295-2870
FTS 752-2870

KENTUCKY
William E. Burnette
333 Waller Ave.
Lexington, KY 40504
(606) 233-2733
FTS 355-2733

LOUISIANA
Nimrod T. Andrews
3727 Government St.
Alexandria, LA 71301
(318) 448-3421
FTS 497-6611

MAINE
Seth H. Bradstreet
USDA Office Bldg.
Orono, ME 04473
(207) 866-4929
FTS 833-7445

MASSACHUSETTS
(Connecticut, Massachusetts,
  Rhode Island)
William E. Curry
358 No. Pleasant St.
Amherst, MA 01002
(413) 549-2820

MICHIGAN
Robert L. Mitchell
Rm. 209
1405 So. Harrison Rd.
East Lansing, MI 48823
(517) 372-1910, Ext. 272
FTS 374-4272

MINNESOTA
John Apitz
252 Federal Office Bldg. &
  Courthouse
316 No. Robert St.
St. Paul, MN 55101
(612) 752-5842
(Use same 7-digit no. for FTS)

MISSISSIPPI
Mark G. Hazard
Rm. 830, Milner Bldg.
Jackson, MS 39201
(601) 969-4316
FTS 490-4316

MISSOURI
Allan H. Brock
555 Vandiver Dr.
Columbia, MO 65201
(314) 442-2271, Ext. 3241
FTS 276-3241

MONTANA
Wallace B. Edland
Federal Bldg.
P.O. Box 850
Bozeman, MT 59715
(406) 587-5271, Ext. 4211
FTS 585-4211

NEBRASKA
Leonard T. Hanks
Rm. 308, Federal Bldg.
100 Centennial Mall No.
Lincoln, NE 68508
(402) 471-5551
FTS 541-5551

NEW JERSEY
Lawrence E. Suydam
1 Vahlsing Center
Robbinsville, NJ 08691
(609) 259-3176
FTS 342-0232

NEW MEXICO
David W. King
Rm. 3414, Federal Bldg.
517 Gold Ave., SW
Albuquerque, NM 87102
(505) 766-2462
FTS 474-2462

NEW YORK
(New York, Virgin Islands)
Karen N. Hanson
Rm. 871
U.S. Courthouse &
  Federal Bldg.
100 So. Clinton St.
Syracuse, NY 13202
(315) 423-5290
FTS 950-5290

NORTH CAROLINA
James T. Johnson
Rm. 514, Federal Bldg.
310 New Bern Ave.
Raleigh, NC 27601
(919) 755-4640
FTS 672-4640

NORTH DAKOTA
Frederick S. Gengler
Rm. 208, Federal Bldg.
For letter mail:
P.O. Box 1737
Bismark, ND 58501
(701) 255-4011
FTS 783-4781

OHIO
Gene R. Abercrombie
Rm. 507, Federal Bldg.
200 No. High St.
Columbus, OH 43215
(614) 469-5606
FTS 943-5606

OKLAHOMA
Gene F. Earnest
Agriculture Center Off. Bldg.
Stillwater, OK 74074
(405) 624-4250
FTS 728-4250

OREGON
Kenneth Keith Keudell
Rm. 1590, Federal Bldg.
1220 SW 3rd Ave.
Portland, OR 97204
(503) 221-2731
FTS 423-2731

PENNSYLVANIA
J. Fred King
Rm. 728, Federal Bldg.
228 Walnut St.
For letter mail:
P.O. Box 905
Harrisburg, PA 17108
(717) 782-4476
FTS 590-4476

PUERTO RICO
Juan Jose Jimenez
Federal Bldg.
Carlos Chardon St.
Hato Rey, PR 00918
For letter mail:
G.P.O. Box 6106G
San Juan, PR 00936
(809) 753-4308
(Use same 7-digit no. for FTS)

SOUTH CAROLINA
Karl G. Smith
240 Stoneridge Rd.
For letter mail:
P.O. Box 21607
Columbia, SC 29221
(803) 765-5876
FTS 677-5876

SOUTH DAKOTA
Jack M. Weiland
Rm. 208
Huron Federal Bldg.
200 Fourth St., SW
For letter mail:
P.O. Box 821
Huron, SD 57350
(605) 352-8651, Ext. 355
FTS 782-2355

TENNESSEE
Earl Wayne Avery
538 U.S. Court House Bldg.
801 Broadway
Nashville, TN 37203
(615) 251-7341
FTS 852-7341

TEXAS
William H. Pieratt
W.R. Poage Bldg.
101 So. Main
Temple, TX 76501
(817) 744-1301
FTS 736-1301

UTAH
(Nevada, Utah)
Reed J. Page
Rm. 5311, Federal Bldg.
125 So. State St.
Salt Lake City, UT 84138
(801) 524-5027
FTS 588-5057

VERMONT
(New Hampshire, Vermont)
Brian D. Burns
141 Main St.
P.O. Box 588
Montpelier, VT 05602
(802) 223-2371
FTS 832-4454

VIRGINIA
Edward A. Ragland
Rm. 8213, Federal Bldg.
400 No. 8th St.
For letter mail:
P.O. Box 10106
Richmond, VA 23240
(804) 782-2451
FTS 925-2451

WASHINGTON
Keith P. Sattler
Rm. 319, Federal Office Bldg.
301 Yakima St.
Wenatchee, WA 98801
(509) 662-4353
FTS 390-0353

WEST VIRGINIA
James Facemire
Rm. 320, Federal Bldg.
For letter mail:
P.O. Box 678
Morgantown, WV 26505
(304) 559-7791
FTS 923-7791

WISCONSIN
Lawrence E. Dahl
P.O. Box 639
Suite 209,
First Financial Plaza
Stevens Point, WI 54481
(715) 341-5900
FTS 360-3889

WYOMING
Rudolph W. Knoll
Federal Bldg.
100 E. B St.
For letter mail:
P.O. Box 820
Casper, WY 82601
(307) 265-5550, Ext. 3272
FTS 328-5271

To locate County Farmers Home Administration Officers, consult your telephone directory under U.S. Department of Agriculture, or the State Office of the Farmers Home Administration listed above.

APPENDIX G

U.S. SECURITIES & EXCHANGE COMMISSION
REGIONAL OFFICES

Region 1   New York and New Jersey

          William D. Moran,
          Regional Administrator
          26 Federal Plaza
          *New York, NY 10007
          (212) 264-1636

Region 2   Maine, New Hampshire, Vermont,
          Massachusetts, Rhode Island,
          Connecticut

          Michael Stewart,
          Regional Administrator
          150 Causeway St.
          Boston, MA 02114
          (617) 223-2721

Region 3   Tennessee, Virgin Islands,
          Puerto Rico, North Carolina,
          South Carolina, Georgia,
          Alabama, Mississippi,
          Florida, Louisiana (east of
          the Atchafalaya River)

          Jule B. Greene
          Regional Administrator
          1375 Peachtree St., NE
          Suite 788
          Atlanta, GA 30309
          (404) 881-2524

          MIAMI BRANCH OFFICE
          William Nortman,
          Assoc. Regional Administrator
          Dupont Plaza Center
          300 Biscayne Blvd. Way
          Suite 1114
          Miami, FL 33131
          (305) 350-5765

Region 4   Michigan, Ohio, Kentucky,
          Wisconsin, Indiana, Iowa, Min-
          nesota, Missouri, Kansas City
          (Kansas), and Illinois

          William D. Goldsberry
          Regional Administrator
          Everett McKinley Dirksen Bldg.
          219 So. Dearborn St., Rm. 1204
          *Chicago, IL 60604
          (312) 353-7390

          CLEVELAND BRANCH OFFICE
          Orazio Sipari
          Attorney-in-Charge
          1020 Standard Bldg.
          1370 Ontario St.
          Cleveland, OH 44113
          (216) 522-4060

          DETROIT BRANCH OFFICE
          Mark A. Loush
          Attorney-in-Charge
          1044 Federal Bldg.
          Detroit, MI 48226
          (313) 226-6070

          ST. LOUIS BRANCH OFFICE
          John F. Kern
          Attorney-in-Charge
          210 No. 12th St., Rm. 1452
          St. Louis, MO 63101
          (314) 425-5555

Region 5   Oklahoma, Arkansas, Texas,
          Louisiana (west of the At-
          chafalaya River) and Kansas
          (except Kansas City)

          Robert M. Hewitt
          Regional Administrator
          503 U.S. Court House
          10th & Lamar Sts.
          Fort Worth, TX 76102
          (817) 334-3393

          HOUSTON BRANCH OFFICE
          Daniel R. Hirshbaum
          Asst. Administrator

Federal Office & Courts Bldg.
515 Rusk Ave., Rm. 5615
Houston, TX 77002
(713) 226-4986

Region 6　North Dakota, South Dakota,
Wyoming, Nebraska, Colorado,
New Mexico, Utah

Robert H. Davenport
Regional Administrator
Two Park Central, Rm. 640
1515 Arapahoe St.
Denver, CO 80202
(303) 837-2071

SALT LAKE BRANCH OFFICE
G. Gail Weggeland
Attorney-in-Charge
Federal Reserve Bank Bldg.
120 So. State St.
Salt Lake City, UT 84111
(801) 524-5796

Region 7　Nevada, Arizona, California,
Hawaii, Guam

Gerald E. Boltz
Regional Administrator
10960 Wilshire Blvd.
Suite 1710
*Los Angeles, CA 90024
(213) 473-4511

SAN FRANCISCO BRANCH OFFICE
Leonard H. Rossen
Assoc. Administrator

450 Golden Gate Ave.
Box 36042
San Francisco, CA 94102
(415) 556-5264

Region 8　Montana, Idaho, Washington,
Oregon, Alaska

Jack H. Bookey
Regional Administrator
3040 Federal Bldg.
915 Second Ave.
Seattle, WA 98174
(206) 442-7990

Region 9　Pennsylvania, Delaware,
Maryland, Virginia, West
Virginia, District of Columbia

Paul F. Leonard
Regional Administrator
Ballston Center Tower 3
4015 Wilson Blvd.
Arlington, VA 22203
(703) 557-8201

PHILADELPHIA BRANCH OFFICE
Thomas H. Monahan
Assistant Administrator
William J. Green, Jr. Federal
　Bldg.
600 Arch St., Rm. 2204
Philadelphia, PA 19106
(215) 597-2278

*Public Reference Room

INDEX